Smiles and I

By Dr. InaNorma Yanez

www.capallbann.co.uk

Smiles and Miracles

©Copyright InaNorma Yanez 2003

ISBN 186163 166 9

ALL RIGHTS RESERVED

Cover design by Paul Mason

Published by:

Capall Bann Publishing
Auton Farm
Milverton
Somerset
TA4 1NE

Contents

Introduction   3

Chapter One Healing   5

Chapter Two Healing Rubyglow   9

Chapter Three A Ferret's Stay of Execution   13

Chapter Four Dead and Buried   17

Chapter Five Healing Through Rhythm   19

Chapter Six Apache's Gift   23

Chapter Seven A Nurse's Observations   25

Chapter Eight The Rescuing Hug   27

Chapter Nine Max's Reprieve   29

Chapter Ten A Bird Named "Miracle"   33

Chapter Eleven Revival From Clinical Death   37

(The Near Death Experience)   37

Chapter Twelve Cardiac Arrest   41

Chapter Thirteen The Operation Was a Success, But
   The Patient Died   45

Chapter Fourteen An Entertainer's Lightning Bolt   49

Chapter Fifteen Psychic Surgery   55

Chapter Sixteen Survival Against All Odds   59

Chapter Seventeen The Many Forms of Healing   65

Chapter Eighteen Nikko's Story   67

Chapter Nineteen Mickey   71

Chapter Twenty Love Me Enough To Let Me Go   73

Chapter Twenty One Our Amazing Animals   77

Chapter Twenty Two Biggie Saved Grandma's Life   79

Chapter Twenty Three Brittany The Feline Heroine   81

Chapter Twenty Four Sammy's Show of Sympathy   83

Chapter Twenty Five Purrrr-Therapy   85

Chapter Twenty Six   Feline Health Intuitive   87

Chapter Twenty Seven Our Cats Take Care of Us   91

Chapter Twenty Eight Nadia's Gift For Healing   93

Chapter Twenty Nine A Father Saves His Daughter's Life   97

Chapter Thirty A Laboratory Experiment In Telepathy   101

Chapter Thirty One Did You See That Apparition Too?   103

Chapter Thirty Two Visits From Spirit   107

Chapter Thirty Three The Visit From Hell   110

Chapter Thirty Four Finding Lost Things With The Help
   of Saint Anthony   115

Chapter Thirty Five When Objects Move by Themselves....   117

Chapter Thirty Six Beware Of Psychic Mis-information
   And Frauds   125

Chapter Thirty Seven The Dream That Saved Lives   127

Chapter Thirty Eight World War Two Psychic Drama   131

Chapter Thirty Nine Archeology And The Paranormal   135

Chapter Forty Did You Ever See A Dream Walking?   140

Chapter Forty One Irene Was My Mother's Name   147

Introduction

Magick and the paranormal events of history have filled people with awe and a mystical feeling since the beginning of time. It has always existed, been discussed, analyzed, and disputed. We have given unexplained events many names. Some call them "miracles." Others refer to the paranormal as "spooky." Whenever delving into these intriguing and exotic subjects my face invariably lights up with a smile. Since miracles do happen and have been reported throughout written history, "Smiles and Miracles" will be the title we give to all the following stories you are about to read. Many of the events discuss people. Some pertain to animals, and most especially to cats. With the best of intentions, these happenings have been authenticated as well as could be accomplished through years of research, in person questioning, sworn testimonials, and my own on site scrutiny. When-ever possible, we observed the accounts given to us by being physically there to do the reporting. Phenomenal healings, Extra Sensory Perception(s), prayer, meditative thoughts plus synchronicity, all play major roles in these researched accounts. Many of those involved have said, "They did not believe in a God." Others were devout in their religiosity.

Perhaps some day we shall understand more fully why such amazing phenomena occur. The purpose of this book is not to explain. It is to report so many events that have been testified to, that you, the reader, will come up with your own comfortable and believable explanations. Sometimes the topics will overlap.

Our sincerest wish is to have more and more reasoning people come to accept the normality of what we term "miraculous healing" and "the paranormal" as every day occurrences. Wherever possible, please take into account that when there is a strong belief system, this in and of itself can affect an outcome. Yet it still does not explain many of the paranormal accounts we were given where no conscious thoughts were involved or attested to.

We shall place our stories in the following general categories of: Healing, Telepathy, and All Other Phenomena. The accounts of people and animals will therefore sometimes inter-mingle. This book can be read in any order. Names and places are altered to keep confidential information private. If genuine names are used, it is with the signed permission of those discussed. We open with "Healing" which does not always mean that a permanent cure occurred.

Chapter One

Healing

Our first story involves a young man in the armed forces. He asked that his name, location, and rank be withheld from the story. For convenience we will call him John. John was working with ten other young men unloading poisons from huge canisters. Suddenly a crash and spill caused the chemicals to leak out on all men involved. John did not know what exactly they were unloading, but a terrible feeling of forboding came over him as the eleven ill-fated men were washing themselves off from the toxic spill. Within six months he developed malignant tumors in both his brain and spinal column.

Chemotherapy and radiation were immediately given. It did not help. Surgery and a change of diet were also prescribed. Nothing helped. More chemotherapy of a different nature was administered along with massive doses of radiation. John died on the table and literally had to be brought back to life from far too much radiation. His doctors sadly had to tell this young suffering man "You are in the last stages of terminal cancer." Then they sent him home to die.

John had heard about a clinic in Mexico that did alternative therapies. Selling everything he owned and borrowing as much as he could because insurance did not cover these treatments, John left for a date with destiny.

The treatments were as follows....

*There was a total change in his diet. It entailed juicing fresh organic fruits and vegetables.
*All proteins were eliminated. John was told "Cancer feeds off proteins."
*Fresh grains, raw nuts, and more herbs than he had any knowledge of were administered daily.
*Chelation therapy, an intravenous solution to clean out the blood, was used over thirty times.
*Twice daily he was hypnotized using guided imagery to vaporize the cancer.
*He meditated a minimum of twice daily for at least thirty minutes at a time.
*Group therapy was given once a day to discuss options in thinking, hugging, and more use of imagination for healing.
*Laughing was frequently used as an actual medication.
*They introduced the use of a modality that has the patient experience Rapid Eye Movement (REM) for the release of traumatic memories. John did not wish to give this treatment a name, but claimed it was very gentle and soothing.
*Discussions on physical death and life after life were frequent. He felt "It removed the fear of dying and made him calm about the outcome of his treatments."
*John was in the clinic for three months and released to go home for medical tests.

When this extraordinary man and I met it was five years after having alternative treatments. He had tested clean from cancer up until his giving the account of suffering and courage to us. John has since married and become involved in the stock market. He has hopes for a normal life lived to the fullest.

John's health has been a vital issue because the chemotherapy treatments and radiation sessions destroyed a great deal of healthy tissue. He wears many permanent scars on his body from serious cancer operations that were performed in an effort to save him. Though the original treatments were meant to help, in his case they caused permanent damage to his bones and muscles. John suffers painful spasms and dislocation of bones. But, after five years has seen no re-occurrence of any form of cancer. When he told me of the long and tortured journey to save his life, we both wept. No one can say with certainty how long anyone has to live. In John's case, these five years have been a priceless gift.

Chapter Two

Healing Rubyglow

When we picked up our beloved Bengal kitten RubyGlow from her breeder, little did we realize what was to come to pass in our personal educations about veterinary emergency medicine. I thought she was on the small side, but was given assurancesthat our kitten's health was perfect. So home we went holding instructions on feeding with premium food, litter box, and other training ideas.

Ruby ate voraciously, but failed to thrive. In a brief time she was at our vet's office and they held out no hope. Her bones were like butter, she could barely walk, and was in obvious terrible pain. In fact, no one was exactly sure what it was that definitely was taking our kitten's life? So they labeled it "The Withering Disease." Our vet suggested we put her down since all seemed futile. RubyGlow was only three months old, suffering terribly, barely able to breathe, stomach distended, and paws malformed from not absorbing nutrients. I took the news very hard, and cried a river of prayers.

While visiting my own doctor I met a woman who had knowledge of breeding English bull dogs. Without knowing why, I began telling her about Ruby's mystery illness. The woman smiled at me, shared that we both had the exact birth date and year, and then strongly advised me to do the following for Ruby....

*Around the clock every twenty minutes for the first four days I rubbed a mixture of strained baby chicken and evaporated

goat's milk on my ailing kitten's teeth for her to osmose through inner lips and gums.

*Then with a plastic oral syringe I administered droplets of pure water into her mouth while her head was held straight not to choke her. The drops were gently and very slowly put into the side of the mouth.

*She was to be held between the north sides of two medical magnets whenever possible for as long as possible.

*We prayed over her and directed our thoughts for "perfect healing" from our minds into her aura and body, which we were to see as inter-connected.

*A Healing Touch practitioner was called in to give RubyGlow two treatments daily for a week. Briefly.... Healing Touch is an ancient but rediscovered modality which works with the electromagnetic energies around all living things. It is presently being used in many hospitals before, during, and post surgical operation by nurse practitioners for wound closure and reduction of swelling and inflammation. There are many other uses for Healing Touch. (We have studied it in depth since then).

After four days I was to call this kind woman and tell her about Ruby's condition. AMAZING, MIRACULOUS, VASTLY IMPROVED..... It was beyond our wildest hopes. There was a visual improvement in her paws of 20% straightening. Time to bring out a camera? We took many photos over the next few months of this turn around. After two weeks she began eating dry kibble for kittens on her own while still being given the elixir of strained baby chicken and evaporated goat's milk. We added to this a combination of healthful nutrients, and took her to our vet thinking he would be amazed. He was.

Today she is the mother of champion Bengals. Her health and vigor are a precious testimony to factors beyond explaining. We share this information with anyone who wishes to know more about how to help an ailing animal that cannot eat and is considered fatally ill. At no time did our helpful lady friend promise Ruby would live. She only suggested this as a hopeful way to attempt to save our kitten.

We were very fortunate and are grateful her treatment succeeded.

The next story is about a similar situation, but tells of a dying ferret.

Chapter Three

A Ferret's Stay of Execution

What do you do when a friend calls up crying and says, "My pet ferret is dying?" It may sound odd to some but this nine year old geriatric ferret meant the world to our dear friend. She feels as if her pets are her beloved children.

Thinking I was rushing over to be there when Otto the ferret died, for some illogical reason I grabbed a jar of strained baby chicken and evaporated goat's milk at the last second. While driving it seemed silly to have brought the emergency food. When the door opened, Otto was icey cold, nearly bald from not eating, in shock with vital organ shutdown of spleen and kidneys.... and appeared moribund. We said a prayer for his soul to go peacefully, and just held him while waiting for the end. Then it filtered into conversation to just rub the elixir on his teeth and let it osmose into him. At this point, what possible harm could it do?

After forty-five minutes of gently feeding him, Otto stirred and began moving. I put him down on the floor and he moved slowly over to the dry kibble cat food and water bowl that had been his mainstay food for most of his life. When the ferret began eating on his own we just watched in awe. This is the same animal that was about to die in our arms. He continued eating and being loved by our friend for another three months (which in a ferret's life-span is quite a long time).

Then one day we received a call that Otto passed peacefully in his sleep.

My friend was so grateful to have the three months with her cherished pet. Luckily, Otto did not suffer during his stay of execution, and all ended in a more acceptable way for our friend, and apparently for Otto too!

Chapter Four

Dead and Buried

Rose W. Lived in Germany during the early part of the twentieth century. She had never been ill, or felt consciously that The Holocaust was coming to destroy the Jewish population. Her family was celebrating a birthday when suddenly Rose fell down in front of the gathering of relatives. She had no pulse, and was dramatically pronounced dead by two separate doctors. This event happened in 1933.

In the Jewish religion burial is done rapidly according to ancient custom. By the following day Rose W. had been buried with the appropriate ceremonies and the stunned family sat Shiva on wooden boxes to show their sorrow for the demise of this young woman. By the fourth day of sitting Shiva something happened to shake the very foundations of her family's belief system.

Rose stumbled into the house where they were observing the bereavement custom. She was covered with dirt, a bit bloody and cut up from her exit from the coffin and climbing out of the crypt, and proceeded to tearfully tell her family and friends the following story while they all rushed to give her water and medical attention.

Although Rose had been pronounced dead she had instead gone into some kind of time-warp state. The following information was given to her by what she described as "Angels." Rose was shown the systematic destruction of her family and friends by the Nazis. Although this is a most profound and attested to story, only Rose W. left Germany in time to save her own life. The rest of her family perished in the concentration camps.

Chapter Five

Healing Through Rhythm

Have you ever been told "You will never walk again." The following drama is about an account I both witnessed and can attest to. While living in south Florida and attending an Afro-Cuban religious party called a "BEMBE" someone came in on crutches wearing steel leg-braces from ankle to groin on both legs. The woman was in horrible pain and visibly winced each time she moved. We all knew her from the university I was attending, as she and I had been classmates for one full year at that time. Pearl had lost control of both her legs because of severe neurological damage. It happened during failed surgery years before. She was legally disabled, and used a special vehicle license plate for handicapped parking.

The music pulsed with a pronounced beat while most of the people began swaying to the Afro-Cuban hypnotic rhythms. In a "bembe," haunting music and drum beats are used to celebrate the love of a religion called "Santeria." It brings forth beautiful ancient melodies and percussion rhythms that can evoke very primal feelings. Old and young alike are respectfully present without age segregation. The "bembes" are a spiritual spectacle of good food, incredible energy, and can sometimes elicit healings and paranormal phenomena.

My friend Pearl was in for a healing and life alteration that would spin our heads from happiness. We formed a Conga-Line to dance. Pearl obviously was not going to participate. Then a very provoking rhythm began. Without warning, she threw both crutches to the side of the room and joined the

Conga-Line shuffling her feet in time with ours. No one really bothered to notice Pearl's dancing because... Someone else had been entranced and was reeling back and forth, taken with a spirit in a wild and ecstatic state of euphoria. It was an old and very fragile appearing short man who was moving as if a tornado had entered his body. By the time this ended, Pearl was walking without a limp and starting to remove the leg braces. It was dramatic and without logical explanation. She no longer requires the use of crutches.

What powerful energy took command of the worshippers? How blessed I am to have been there to see and know that healing comes in many forms to people fromevery ethnic and religious background. The remarkable energy has no prejudice or racial boundaries. It is not limited to being inside of a church, mosque or synagogue. One's bank accounts aren't in question either. In fact, not a cent was paid or donated by Pearl. She had the courage to come and something divine and wonderful obeyed a universal law we still cannot fully comprehend. For those at the party, it was a normal happening. They credit "THE ORISHAS" who are like saints in their ancient African religion of Santeria.

Chapter Six

Apache's Gift

Apache was wounded so severely he required 164 stitches to close him up. The dog got caught in a wire fence and in trying to get out was ripped to pieces. His owners were distraught, and the vet was hesitant about the prognosis.

When we met him all he could do was lay down and whimper. Apache could not walk and literally had to lay in his faeces until it was removed off the soft blanket. The family had never seen or heard of Healing Touch. I asked them to move the injured dog gently onto their magnetic horse blanket. We all held hands in a circle around Apache and began to pray for healing. It is unclear how long this went on but I'm guessing it was about fifteen minutes. Then all eight of us focused our attention and energy onto the dog. We had decided not to ask for Apache to live. Instead we asked for "perfect healing" and were allowing whatever fate might bring. After what felt like forty five minutes we broke the circle and sat down for some tea. I showed the family as many practical moves of Healing Touch that I knew might help and went home. We arrived to hear a message left on the answering machine saying, "Apache got up from the magnetic horse blanket and walked with a terrible limp to eat his food." No one had done any of the Healing Touch moves on him yet. The family worked for a few hours in shifts. By the next day Apache's limp had somewhat diminished. It is two years now and the lucky dog has improved to the point of barely limping.Their veterinarian was amazed at his unexpected improvement.

Chapter Seven

A Nurse's Observations

The following stories were sent to us by a nurse. She had so many documented accounts of miraculous-like healings we did not know which to choose from her generous contributions. Thank you so much Pat.

On November 9th, 1969, in Lake Charles, Louisiana, Pat was working in the newborn division nursery at Lake Charles Memorial Hospital. A baby was born weighing only one pound nine ounces. With just twenty three weeks of gestation, there seemed to be no hope for saving the little one's fragile life. At no time were extraordinary measures taken that are often used today. Because of an infection though, at one point she was given a scalp vein IV. This was to help prevent dehydration. The baby was on an apnea monitor and was placed in an incubator, but that was it! Her delivery was such an emergency that sterile conditions were not available either. According to Pat, this baby was something amazing to behold.

She would watch the tiny infant turn over and pull the Dixie cup, with an oxygen tube in it, closer to her little body. When it was not needed any more, the baby pushed it away again. Every day Pat had this shift she prayed for the baby both in person as well as away from the hospital. Never in her career had she seen an infant behave like this before. (Most especially one fighting so valiantly to live).

Pat recalls that this was a small hospital with no neo-natal ICU. It was the baby herself that was the miracle, not the technology. In fact, she told me "You can get a legal abortion up to twenty four weeks into a pregnancy because at twenty-three weeks a baby is just not considered viable."

When the amazing little girl went home she was a mere five pounds. It was two and a half months before she was able to leave the hospital, and still before her due date. It should have been a given that she would be blind because of all the oxygen that was administered. Yet she could see.

Pat had a life altering experience from the child's courage. So the miracle enticed yet another miracle in the nurse's personal life. She credits this exceptional child as a vivid blessing, and never has been the same since. Even in the most serious of medical cases, Pat urges people to continue praying and keep on hoping until it's over, one way or another. The baby somehow fed off this nurse's prayers, energy, and loving intentions.

Chapter Eight

The Rescuing Hug

Along these same lines of infant courage and wisdom, we have a brief and moving story of twins....

In their first week of life the twins were having a vastly different beginning from one another. Apparently each baby was in their respective incubators, with one of them not expected to live.

A hospital nurse fought against the hospital's rules and placed the babies in a single incubator. When they were put together the healthier of the two threw an arm over her sister in an endearing embrace. With this act of love, the smaller baby's heart rate stabilized and her temperature rose to normal.

In reading this story I realize that the babies came from one egg. What cosmic ties they had to begin with! While one was languishing the other instinctively knew to touch her sister and somehow rekindle the life force. Once the nurse chose to use her own courage in the life saving action to put them together, their future was dramatically altered.It was completely against the rules and yet in the nurse's experienced mind, this brave act was what she chose to do. The courage she had to buck the system for a dying baby is an act of unselfish caring. How many of us would have done the same thing?

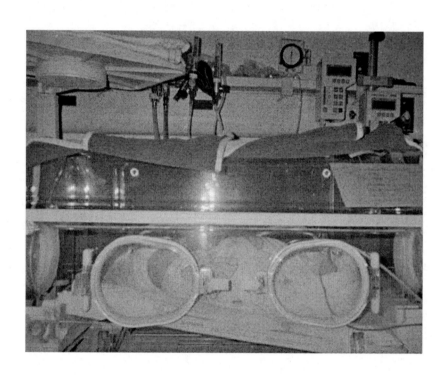

Chapter Nine

Max's Reprieve

When I first heard about Max from his owner, it was in a chiropractor's office. The doctor's assistant, Rifka, was a great animal lover with quite a few pets. Rifka was always telling patients about her special dog Max. He was loved by so many people for his endearing antics, high intelligence, and wonderful temperament.

I returned for treatments after an absence of one year to sadly hear that Max had taken a terrible turn in his health. Rifka's vet could only suggest to put the dog to sleep. He was unable to walk on his own and she had to work full time for a living. When she came home from the office, her dog Max would be lying in his own excrement and obviously in pain from advanced bone deterioration. Although the family was heart broken about having to put their precious sixteen year old pet to sleep, they set the sad date for September 21st, at 9:00a.m. She told me this information the day before, on September 20th. I left and went home with a heavy heart for my friends. That evening, I sent out e-mails to a long list of people who pray for others. In fact, it was twenty people to whom I wrote. They in turn contact others around the world creating a prayer ring. My request for this lovely family and Max was, "To have a smooth transition with as little suffering as possible for all concerned."

About three months later I went back to visit my chiropractor and his assistant Rifka. I chose my words carefully knowing Max's last day on earth would be brought up in conversation.

Well, was I in for a wonderful story!

Rifka told me how the alarm clock went off at 7:00a.m. that morning and all the family did to get ready for his appointment. They fed the other animals and then went in to see their beloved pet Max. He was nowhere in sight. After a long search they found him walking in their back yard. The doggie/kittie door led outside. He had to use the yard to go "pottie." What a shock and joyous event all at the same time. Max was actually walking on his own. He still limped, but for some wondrous reason which no one could figure out, the dog was given another chance to live.

Needless to say, the vet happily took the cancelled appointment without anything but awe in his own voice. I went without contact with them for those few months until the day I decided to visit Rifka. When the story was told to me I began smiling. Then they were in for another surprise because I discussed the prayer circle that spread the word around the world to pray for Max and his human family. Each of us is to contact twenty people who then will contact another twenty people exponentially. It is impossible to know how many were actually sending out healing thoughts on behalf of Max's situation that September 20th. Fortunately, it seems enough kind souls were contacted to bring about a big change in one family's life.

Rifka, her boss the chiropractor, and the receptionist were not a bit flustered about the use of prayer for healing. In fact it made perfect sense to them. How nice to hear of this three months later instead of being told Max was put to sleep. And, what a good feeling it gave me to know that so many tried to help a total stranger.

Chapter Ten

A Bird Named "Miracle"

How many times have I looked at birds and taken them for granted? After all, there are so many of them flying, chirping, and pooping up our car windows. This was about to be changed when we discovered a newborn bird lying so helplessly in our front yard.

Thinking we should try to put it under a shaded tree where many other birds were chirping, we did so in the hope that the mother would scoop it up back to the nest.I kept walking outside looking to see what was happening to the wee one. Well it disappeared from under the tree. Great, I thought. It is back with the mom.

No such luck. It was now under my daughter's car in our carport far away from the tree where we had placed it. The baby was lying in the shade with some kind of bird wisdom I was just about to begin appreciating. Please realize that it was so fragile and delicate, having nearly no feathers. Again, we put it under the tree praying for its parents to come for it.

After dinner, we went out and the bird was not in sight. On a hunch, I looked under the car. YIKES! There it was lying right next to a rear wheel. We had to get it out since my daughter was running to do an evening medical shift at her school's clinic.

Once I got the bird under some light, it was obvious it had a totally deformed left leg. Was this why it was out of its nest?

Did the natural instinct of the mother or father know to get rid of it since it was already not perfect enough to survive by their bird standards? Yet this baby was fighting with a spirit to live that forced me to name it "MIRACLE."

My daughter and I decided to fight along with it to keep it alive if possible. We made some calls and learned we could give the bird moist, scrambled eggs as well as softened pellets of kitten food. Prying its mouth open was a great challenge that worked best with two people. We splinted its deformed leg so it wouldn't further injure it. Every four to six hours either I alone or my daughter and I repeated this routine for the following three days. The day before my daughter's birthday, "Miracle" started to rally. He/she became hyper-active and gobbled up food and water valiantly. At this point we were about to take it to a bird sanctuary.

I came home to find a very interesting situation. When it was in the car and with the ignition on, "Miracle" telepathically begged not to be taken away from our home. It was as if the baby bird could speak its own mind. What an uncanny little life-form, with the courage of many, we had the naive responsibiliy of trying to help. After its last miniscule meal and hydration, I patted the precious dime-sized head, said a prayer, and went to sleep. From the very beginning we gave it permission to cross over THE RAINBOW BRIDGE when and if it was supposed to die.

The next morning I awoke feeling like my soul had been treated to a major lesson while sleeping. When I went to take care of the baby bird, it had gone to another realm. It was so peaceful in death. And so beautiful in its courage and wisdom too.

"Miracle" somehow knew when we were taking it away to the bird sanctuary to tell us it preferred to stay here when it died. We were the ones who had loved and nurtured it around the clock, even though it was severely maimed and deformed. We were also the family it imprinted with. I buried this amazingly brave creature with our dead litter of kittens in a pretty sanctuary we made in our backyard. It is a place of meditation, beautiful palms and citrus trees, where we placed many exotic stones and minerals. When the bells ring softly in the breeze, I can almost feel the spirit of our little "Bird Named Miracle." It has been a lesson in courage above and beyond anything I have personally witnessed before. Bless you and thank you "Miracle" for coming into our lives. And now you can truly fly with the angels. amen

Chapter Eleven

Revival From Clinical Death

(The Near Death Experience)

In discussing The Near Death Experience, now to be known as "NDE" we are not pushing any personal opinions on you. It is a phenomenon that is so heated and controversial, even the most educated people of science and religion keep arguing over what this is really about. Instead, we shall report the experiences people have related to us over the years with their own words, memories and feelings.

DROWNING.... Lara was an exceptionally good swimmer, diver, and.... a smoker. One day she decided to dive into the community pool for a swim. Unfortunately,Lara never surfaced. This is her story about the adventure of a lifetime, while she drowned. Lara did not heed years of bodily warnings like shortness of breath, constant coughing, and pain in her lungs. When she deftly dove into the pool that sunny summer day, Lara had no idea a fateful force above and beyond her control was at play.

While at the bottom of the ten foot deep pool, she did her normal examination of the floor. It still needed a painting and the chips were obvious. Suddenly, Lara realized it was time to surface. But the energy required to accomplish this was not there. The more she tried, the more calm Lara became. It was at first eerie, then very peaceful. She knew enough not to try to inhale as the water would kill her.

And then Lara realized she was dying!

A myriad of movie-like films began to flash before her eyes. It was just like being in a theater. Lara was shown every conceivable memory of her life that the human mind could conjure up. All the scenes were in living color, vivid beyond words, in timed sequence of the events, and full with vital information her conscious mind had long ago forgotten. And.... they were in three dimensional spatial view, meaning she could reach out to touch the figures and objects as if they were actually there with her in their totality of existence. The sounds that came with this event were bigger than life, and full spectrumed. Even smells were available as well as tactile experiences. Every event that passed by Lara's eyes, ears, nose, mouth, and sense of touch, was one that had occurred in her life which was of significance. Absolutely nothing that ever mattered was left out. The time for all this to have taken place could not have exceeded more than three to five minutes maximum. Yet, it encompassed a full thirty-nine years of her life memories here on earth.

One of the astounding feelings that remained ever-present in Lara's NDE was that at no time did she experience fear. In fact, she claims, "It was the most beautiful thing that ever happened to me."

After her entire life flashed before her, Lara has no more recall other than passing through a long tunnel and seeing indescribable brilliant light. With a terrible pain in her chest, lungs, head, and violent nausea, Lara found herself being worked on by an assortment of professional lifesavers. The lifeguard, para-medics, and onlookers were positive she had died. Her vitals were gone. Yet, because she was young, and so many at the pool knew her personally, they continued trying to bring Lara back to life.

The next thing she remembers is being embarrassed that all the neighbors had to see her humiliating struggle. The ego kicked in. According to those who had worked on Lara, she was "clinically dead." According to Lara, she was more alive than ever while in that other dimension and having such vivid recalls with all her senses.

From that day forward she never smoked another cigarette. The NDE triggered a dramatic attitude change. Lara began college, became involved with helping others quit life-threatening habits, and tells anyone who will sincerely listen about her Near Death Experience.

Chapter Twelve

Cardiac Arrest

When Shirley was wheeled into the hospital during the summer of 1941, no one ever dreamed she would die giving birth to her first baby.

Shirley went into labor and immediately began cleaning her apartment. She thought nothing of this extraodinary spasm of physical energy other than wanting to come home from the hospital to a clean place. Besides, she was always filled with more "pizazz" to do hard physical work than most. Her health was excellent. In fact, the doctor was very surprised that during the nine months she had not gained too much weight at all. She left her sparkling clean apartment to deliver the new baby almost with a smile, in between the labor pains.

Upon arrival at the hospital, they determined she was nearly ready to deliver. Yet, the baby did not come. It was a time when c-section surgery was considered a life and death procedure in and of itself. Why they let her go for three days and nights no one can understand? Suddenly, Shirley was dead. Her heart stopped from the agony of hard labor which went on relentlessly for so long. After seventy-two hours, the woman in her mid-twenties who had entered the hospital in top health, had a complete stoppage of her heart function!

With the young woman's life ended, came a frantic effort to revive her and remove the full-term baby surgically before it died too. The delivery room turned into a volcano of action.

While the baby was being released from its home of nine months, Shirley experienced another state of consciousness.

This is her story written in the first person....

"Well, all of a sudden I stopped hurting and screaming in hard labor pain. What a relief. I thought the baby had finally come out and that was why the agony ended. But then I saw a field of daisies. It was the most beautiful thing you could imagine. The hues were more brilliant than anything I ever saw before. I thought about this for a second and could not understand what these flowers were doing in the delivery room of a hospital? Then I heard or sensed a voice speaking to me. It did not seem to be male or female. The neutral voice was very gentle and called me to leave with it. I was not afraid, nor was I anxious to go. It certainly was a strange feeling to be mentally torn in both directions at the same time.

Something drew me to leave with this voice, while something else pulled me to remain in the hospital. Even though none of this was making any sense, I just floated in the glory of those flowers and the sense of freedom the gorgeous field seemed to bestow on me. Part of my reasoning did not wish to return to the pain. Another portion of me yearned to see my baby grow up. And.... my heart wanted to journey and seek out heaven.

The next thing I knew, it was very dark. I felt a bed under me and knives cutting my guts out. It hurt beyond any words I could find to describe the torture. Was this death? Somehow, they had revived me. Don't ask how many incisions my body had endured or what I was experiencing, because even today, so many years later, it makes me ill. People were standing over me saying, "It was a miracle." I had been unconscious for four days. Tubes were sticking out wherever my eyes looked. I was a mess, but according to them, "A living miracle." No pain-killers worked on me, and I hated these medical people. They were nothing but sadists in white clothes.

Or.... perhaps it was helping but the pain would have have been far worse without the drugs? I thought about the poor baby. Did it live? But my mouth was frozen and unable to speak yet. More days went by in a blur of agony. Finally I could move my mouth to ask for the baby. She lived but had been seriously injured in the dangerous delivery. They did not know what was wrong with her but she was failing to thrive. It would take another two years for the little one to finally leave the hospital and go home."

The story of this baby girl's fight to survive against all odds, will be told in a later segment of our discussion on "Miracles, Healing and Extra Sensory Perception."

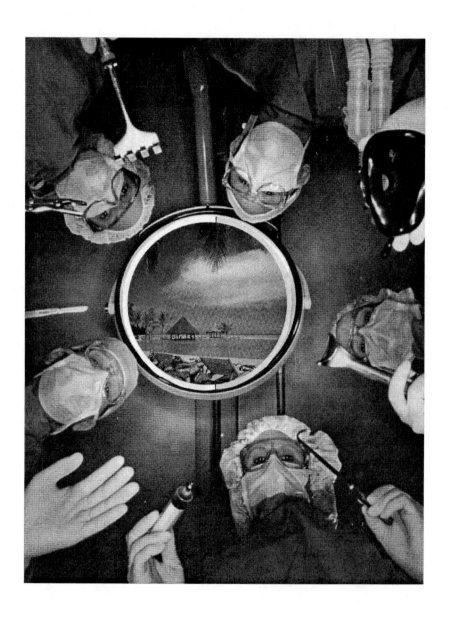

44

Chapter Thirteen

The Operation Was a Success, But The Patient Died

How many times has this title been said in semi-jest? But for Angel, it was exactly what happened....

Angel was no stranger to hardships. She had been operated on many times in her young life. This was a woman with the spirit of many. When she arrived for the experimental operation to save her kidney, there was not a shred of cowardice or fear. It was just another operation in a teaching hospital, and would all become a memory soon enough. Hadn't every other surgery been this way? Her courage was a great asset. Angel shared the hospital room with a very old and fragile cardiac patient, as well as another lady who had the curtain drawn.

Curiousity got the best of Angel the evening before her surgery was to take place. She asked a nurse what was wrong with the lady inside the drawn curtain area, and was told the patient had no family, and had fallen into a coma from terminal cancer. Angel thought, "What sick partners to share this sad hospital room with."

Some muffled noises came from the drawn curtain area, so she went to see for herself a person who was dying. Angel found a mute emaciated female who seemed able to speak with her eyes. She mentally told Angel about the devastating thirst and immediately Angel brought over a glass of water with a straw in it. She held the lady who weighed next to nothing at this time and they both struggled to get some liquid into her. It was profound. It was also very lonely because no one was there to help her cross over to the next plane. The dying woman looked directly into Angel's eyes, took a whisper of a breath, and expired there in her arms.

What Angel experienced was an immediate sensation that the woman's body weight became lighter. Then a shadow of smokey air-like substance left from the top of the deceased lady's head. Holding her dead body, Angel began to think about what to do next. She had one dead person next to her and the other woman could easily have a heart attack if she knew what just transpired. It was a dilemma Angel had to think out with her unusual courageous spirit. She gently placed the woman (who now appeared so serene) onto the pillow, covered her face with the blanket, and hobbled to the nursing station. Angel had been given many sedatives to calm her before tomorrow's scheduled kidney operation, and was feeling weak and fragile herself. Yet she managed to get over to the nurses and let them know about the lady with the heart condition being totally unaware of the corpse in her room. The staff handled this situation by closing off all the patients' doors and rolling the deceased cancer victim outside without speaking or showing any signs that she was dead.

After a surprisingly restful but brief night's sleep Angel herself, was wheeled into surgery. Many more astonishing events were to come to pass for our heroine....General anesthesia was administered. Angel recalls the following with a vivid and doctor verified account of what transpired during the eight hours of surgery.

At first it seemed that all was actually going well. Her vital signs were good. The needed incisions and other assorted medical procedures required for such a surgical endeavor were being completed on schedule. The mood in the operating room also seemed pleasant enough from the combined attending doctors and nurses. But then, it happened. Angel inexplicably began to fail rapidly.

All the while this was going on, she heard, saw, and understood the surgery was taking place. When the medical staff began their arduous effort of saving her from death, she could hear them say...."We're losing her." Again she heard them say, "She's gone." After this Angel seemed to fly out of her body but remained in the room to observe. One of the nurses said she was "nauseated and faint" then the woman passed a large loud wind, and quickly left the operating room. It should have been funny for the exasperated medical co-workers, except they were struggling to retrieve a twenty year old girl back from the clutches of death....

The day passed with Angel flying from underneath the operating table and seeing the socks, shoes, and shoe cover-ups they were wearing, to above the bright ceiling lights illuminating what was now her own clinically dead body. She was a terribly ugly color. Foam was dripping from the side of her mouth and the grey-ish yellow cast of her skin was deepening. Then her face morphed into a movie screen. She was shown many events of her life, from the past to the present to the time of eventual death at age eighty-six. Yes, Angel was told it would be eighty-six.

The girl did not awake until five days had passed. Her young and concerned physician was sitting by her bedside. Did he regret having asked her to be a guinea pig for this experimental operation? Angel opened her eyes and the first thing she innocently gasped was, "How is the nauseous dizzy nurse who farted in the operating room?" The doctor fell off his chair. When asked, "How it was possible for a dead person to have known this?" Angel answered, "You thought I was dead, but I was alive some place else with full consciousness."

It has been over three decades since "The surgery that was a success, but killed its patient." Angel has never required another operation since.

Chapter Fourteen

An Entertainer's Lightning Bolt

For many years Tiana had been suffering with trick knees. They simply would not stay intact, and she had many episodes of finding herself falling down without warning. There were also other times when the warning would come with a severe knifing pain to the knees. Either way, when she underwent reconstructive surgery on both legs, no one had prepared her for the possibility that the surgeries could be a failure and leave the afflicted legs in far worse condition than they were prior to these operations. The worst case scenario happened. Her legs became paralyzed from the knees down with one particular problem added to this negative situation. Now, there was drop foot in both legs. It caused the feet to just dangle, and not have pliability. Tiana did not let this stop her from working in her beloved craft as a professional singer and musician. What it did do, was to sadly and completely end her career as a professional dancer.

The first part of "Tiana's Healing" came when the two doctors who performed the surgeries told her she "Could never walk again." Tiana had been trained in classical ballet. It was this discipline which helped her to learn to walk again.

At first Tiana could not even move her legs. After a torturous few months, some motion returned, but not enough for her to stand. Still relying on dragging herself around on crutches

and a wheelchair, she made up her mind to find a way out of being disabled. The struggle was one of excruciating nerve damage pain, frustration, and depression. Nonetheless, she devised a routine to bring life back to the legs all by herself. There were no helpers, no family, and no physical therapists. Tiana was flat broke to boot. It was a Herculean task.

Sometimes she would literally pass out from the effort of making the legs move. Other times she would push until she broke down sobbing. But she never once thought of quitting. In fact, her sole purpose in life was to regain the ability to walk.

After two years Tiana could walk, exercise, work, and barely show a limp. She went back to see her negative doctors. One had died from a brain tumor. It was revealed by his affiliates that he had done many surgeries while dying from cancer. This was a shock to her system. She was initially filled with rage and a sense of having been betrayed. How many others had this irresponsible man killed or maimed? And..... ironically, he was known as, and considered to be a famous and caring doctor. Did he even realize the harm he caused before his own death?

The wisdom to let it go eventually came after a number of years. Tiana lived her life performing. Then she decided to have a baby. As the weight increased, her legs' ability to hold her decreased. She found herself falling in front of a car one day with absolutely no advance warning. It was a nightmare of worrying that both she and her baby would die because the knees went sour again.

One evening she was entertaining in a nightclub. Downstairs housed a stage, bar, and food. Upstairs was the bathroom. She struggled to drag herself up the stairs to go to the ladies room with both hands holding the railing. When Tiana got to the top she looked down and was terrified. The descent would be even more dangerous and painful than pulling her growing body upstairs. Tiana was five months pregnant, and struggling with the effort to do flights of stairs.

At her wit's end with the pain and fear, she began to pray. She asked for a miracle to safeguard herself and the baby from harm. All her motherly instincts were kicking in from this dangerous drama.

Time felt like an eternity but she prepared herself to go down the stairs with a newly found courage. Suddenly, there was a smoldering bolt of lightning that went from her head through her toes and out her shoes. It was clearly visible and very painful. The lightning shocked her so that a scream left Tiana's lips. Looking downstairs at the waiters and club patrons she was surprised to realize that no one else seemed to be acknowledging the lightning bolt.

"What is going on here? Have I flipped out from stress?" These thoughts came and went when.... an even bigger surprise was about to enter this lady's life. She moved to go down the dreaded staircase and there was zero pain in her legs, knees, and feet. Tiana took another step. Again, there was no pain.

Five trips later the entire population of the crowded nightclub was gawking in disbelief at this pregnant crazy lady going up and down like a marathon runner. She must have been a strange and comical sight in her elegant floor length beaded maternity gown. Finally, the owner went over and asked if she needed help. She was speechless and glassy-eyed with uncontrolled happiness.

Tiana had once more received a gift from somewhere in our eternal universe that simply could not be explained with any traditional logic. What was the mysterious lightning bolt? Why did no other person see it? How could this energy help an unborn baby and mother-to-be? Where did it come from in the first place? Tiana's life had witnessed yet another miracle of healing. She received an uncanny energy that wasn't even remotely possible from a medical standpoint.

Not once did this happen, but twice.

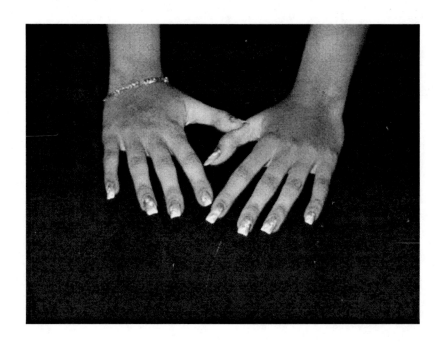

Chapter Fifteen

Psychic Surgery

How difficult it is for a responsible physician to have to tell a person "You are terminally ill. The tumors have spread too far to have much hope. Go home and put your affairs in order."

Dr. Schwartz looked deeply into his patient's eyes. There was trust and respect shining back at him from Morgana's face. Hadn't he delivered her, seen the girl through all her childhood diseases, and now was preparing to give the extensive test results to this stunning young woman? What a blow for Morgana and the family. They were such outstanding people. How many times had they prayed for others during these years when a request had been made? Oh, to get these words out would be painful. "Morgana" he said, "I have some unpleasant news to tell you. Please sit down."

It was two days before she could find the strength to get her family together in one room. They had been nagging her for answers. How long could she put them off? Morgana had been bleeding profusely and did not confide this information to a soul. It was her little tough-luck secret. When she went to Dr. Schwartz for tests, there was a part of her that understood the gravity of profuse vaginal bleeding. But malignant tumors were quite another story. She stalled for a while but then heeded her doctor's advice to set a date for surgery. July 13th was as good as any, and very soon. So it would be July 13th that they open her to remove all hope of ever having a child. Morgana would have loved children. But that was now officially over. What would they find? How many? How far did they spread? This was such a frightening reality that it seemed to be taking the very breath from her body.

"O.K. everybody" Morgana said softly. "All tests show it is advanced cancer." After the shock of these words came through to the Lindquist family, the next thing they could talk about was going to worship, and praying. With heavy hearts and a determination to take this serious matter to GOD, they formed a prayer circle. Not only did they do this in person, but they asked everyone they knew who had a computer to send out a request for "Morgana to be perfectly cured." No one knows exactly how many people ended up being involved in the prayer for Morgana. Be assured there were thousands.

The next person she had to tell was her boyfriend. Actually, Morgana had become engaged recently, but was not sure anymore about getting married, let alone having children, or for that matter, even surviving the cancer. He was a very loving and reasonable man. This was going to hurt them both terribly. But within hours of discussing the medical reports with her family, Morgana now found herself telling the brief details all over again to her husband-to-be. Val's support for her came immediately, and with zero hesitation. He would be with her during all the future chemotherapy and radiation treatments and boldly told Morgana that.... "You will lick this and be fine."

"I will lick this and be fine. I will lick this and be fine." Over and over she repeated these words to herself. Just as long as I can keep on saying it, I'll be safe from dying. It became her constant mantra. Sleep was almost impossible for the first few days after Dr. Schwartz gave her his impression of the disease. Finally, in sheer exhaustion, she went to sleep and had a profound and painful dream. Some would call it a "lucid dream" in which the person who is having the experience feels it is more real than life itself.

In this dream Morgana underwent actual surgery. She could not see who was performing the operation. It really hurt. No anesthesia was administered, nor were the people in the room dressed in hospital garb. She saw herself bleeding, and was shown lumps of tissue that were being removed from her prone body. No one saida word to Morgana during this episode. The entire process was done in complete silence, yet all were able to communicate with each other telepathically. She wrote down the date and exact details after awakening. Then sealed it in an envelope.

Time passed and Morgana chose to keep the dream her own secret. Everyone kept praying while she continued her mantra of "I will lick this and be fine." Soon, it was time to pack a suitcase for her fateful surgery. Morgana entered the hospital, checking in one full day earlier for the required pre-op testing, and made mental preparations for whatever was to be the outcome. Up to the last moment before she was put to sleep, her family continued praying for healing and a miracle. Morgana could hear their words deep inside of her soul. It gave a great sense of being loved.

Nothing could prepare Dr. Schwartz for what he and his surgical assistants found when they opened up Morgana's body. Nothing! No tumors, no growths, only normal looking tissue. Just to be safe they again removed samples for immediate biopsying. It was done with great haste as the doctor had urgently requested.

When all the tests came back negative, they closed her body neatly and swiftly, leaving her totally intact. She and Val are now the parents of a lovely young daughter.They know they were given a priceless treasure. And yes, Dr. Schwartz did deliver their baby.

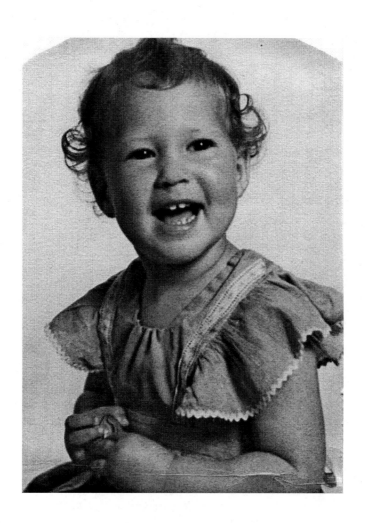

Chapter Sixteen

Survival Against All Odds

A few stories ago, we wrote about a baby who lived her first two years of life in a hospital. The baby's mother Shirley died delivering her and was luckily resuscitated from an NDE (Near Death Experience). The following account is this child's struggle for survival against all odds. It is written in the first person as dictated from Lilly's own words....

"The way I found out that I was born under severe and traumatic circumstances was always hush hush. Apparently, my family thought it was not necessary to discuss such matters with me. I had always been a very sickly little girl and they tried to shelter me so much. My insatiable curiosity taught me to ask innocent looking questions at an early age. Little by little I was able to piece together their remnant answers to form a story about my personal struggle to survive against very tough odds.

There was absolutely no recall of being in the hospital for the first two years of my life. Not until I was studying psychology in college did I learn the real truth about my birth. Natural memory did not kick in until I was a little over two. My lonely childhood was one of frequent and serious illnesses, very unnatural high fevers, and pain. You name it and I caught it. This was the basis for my family being so overly protective. I couldn't go out and play like a normal child. Be careful. I always had to be extra cautious. It made me so angry at times. And I was also very isolated.

There would be long periods when I could not attend school. Once it lasted a full three months. That time was because of an acute ear infection that caused me to temporarily go profoundly deaf. I should probably have been left back.

Being left back that year would have helped me with all the subsequent years of suffering in school from the many studies I had missed in those three months. Most especially was math. From then on math was my nemesis. Unfortunately, my folks were not on top of my foundational education. Anyway, I still got through school.

By the time I was nine, life had offered me eleven serious operations. I was an old pro at being sliced to pieces. It did one special and often remarked upon thing for me though. This forced me to become mentally courageous about dying. They called me "An old soul." In some ways I really was because of the incredible amount of physical suffering. But this enabled me to develop in other ways too. For example, I became a very fine comic. Life was so awful and serious that creating laughter was my most helpful tool for getting past the illnesses."

After what seemed to be the longest drawn out childhood on record, Lilly found herself leaning in the direction of becoming a health professional. While studying a trauma release modality which required the use of hypnosis, Lilly discovered the real truth about how she was born. When she volunteered to have a hypnotic regression session in front of a legion of other students in a large medical school auditorium, the experiences and memories that were elicited from her brought many of the seasoned professionals observing the class to tears.

Lilly recalls.... "I wanted to volunteer for regression so my grade would be higher. They had indicated this to us and I was game for seeking high marks and excelling in school. I walked to the stage and the facilitator asked me to sit on a stool while he began the procedure of inducing a very light hypnotic trance. It felt pleasant and quite safe until....

He asked me to "Go to a time I wanted to heal." Instead of finding the familiar three dimensional world, I zoomed back into a watery lagoon-like environment where it seemed to be warm and cozy. I felt like I was floating and weightless. Could this be heaven, another lifetime, or even another dimension? Then I seemed to hear what sounded like a heart beating very rapidly. Was that my heart? Little by little I understood that I had gone back to my mother's womb.

Wow! What a strange feeling to realize that this is what I came from. It was my home, my shelter, and about to become my tomb. There was an instinctive understanding that both she and I were in grave trouble. Don't ask me how I could fathom this because the answer is not there for you. I just knew. Anyway, something kept crushing me over and over again in my squooshy shelter....

The facilitator required me to look at what it was and to my amazement, it was my mother's right pelvic bone which simply would not open to allow me to be born. It was completely locked closed. The more the pushing action went on, the more I got crushed. A new reality came to me that my mother was dying. During this dramatic hypnotic session it became clear just exactly why mom died. Her heart was being butchered by the stress of hard labor going on for much too long. The torture was not limited to her. I was in great pain too. Then the noise of her heart just stopped as if it had been removed from her body. I also stopped.

All that had been sustaining me throughout our mutual pregnancy had halted. I had nothing to breathe or survive on any longer. Mommy had died, and so did I.

The facilitator had me look around to see where I was after my mother's heart stopped. I saw and felt the presence of something sweet and kind. It loved me unconditionally and said "You could stay if you want to." Then it told me "I had the choice to return if I chose the lessons this little baby girl would have to endure and learn from." What courage did I have to make these choices? I wanted help in deciding but it was not there for me. All choices were mine. Those were the rules. I did not understand where I was, nor did their crazy rules make sense. Perhaps this was another kind of hospital that dead babies go to? Nonetheless, a decision was made. I asked to return.

The following two years contained a series of medical mistakes, ignorance on the part of my doctors, and great tragedy for me. They dried up my mother's milk with a needle because at that time it was considered disgusting for a woman to nurse. I was allergic to all foods. Absolutely no one touched me and they would not allow my mother to handle or caress me because I was so fragile. At birth I weighed 9 and 1/2 pounds. At one year I weighed 9 and 1/2 pounds. My body withered and completely failed to thrive. These people shunned me because I was so sickly.

Because no one touched me.... and they dried up the only source of nutrition that would not have caused violent vomiting (my own mother's milk), I literally starved. What ever sustained me is a total mystery.

When my mother came to see me in the hospital, she would sob uncontrollably. No one else ever showed up. My father seemed to despise me for being weak. Besides, he came from a background that only valued males. So he stopped his visits completely once it became obvious that I would die. The hospital was costing him too much money. In later years, he reminded me of this more than a few times.

The nurses pitied me, but were instructed not to handle my body except to change a diaper or administer medications. I woke up many times in my own blood. Finally, and without warning, I died again. This time at age one. They gave me the last rights, and then I fluttered back once more to the hospital to continue the same old routines. One day my mother was literally running through the hospital hallways screaming for help when a famous baby specialist tried to calm her down. He told her that "If she would permit him to attend me he would either save my life or help it to end without anymore pain." Trust me, there was plenty more pain, but I had no way of telling them.

At two, without hair on my head, or weight on my body, I was released into my family's care from the hospital. Apparently, the doctor had realized that touching was integral to my survival. He would come in and hold me, give my entire body gentle massages, and talk to me with loving words. What a wise and great man he was. He had read a book about the subject of touching written by a world famous medical anthropologist. It taught him that a baby must be touched to thrive.

Thank you Doctor C. for believing Ashley Montague's theory on touching. Despite every indicator saying I would die in that desolate place, this sensitive man, more than anyone else, saw to it that the chance to survive would be mine. He acted more like a father than anyone I've ever known. And he remained my doctor for many years thereafter. I bless you for caring."

Slowly Lilly came out of the trance which allowed her the vision to find out the true introduction to her life here on earth. The facilitator, who had seen many unusual stories evolve from hypnosis, was moved by how much the baby struggled to live. Lilly remained shaking and giving off electric shocks for the next two hours. She was forced to leave the auditorium in order to compose herself. The hidden memories had finally come alive even though those who should have and could have helped her with this vital information chose not to divulge it. Who knows, maybe they were actually trying to protect her from the suffering she went through.

There would be many subsequent sessions for Lilly to deal with her traumatic birth. The health issues that ensued from being crushed almost to death have been partially resolved. She describes the process as "Peeling layers off an onion." In the end, she has become a sensitive and intuitive counselor and therapist for others. Once, when I asked Lilly what good had come from this childhood, she replied, "Well.... I have absolutely no fear of dying."

Chapter Seventeen

The Many Forms of Healing

Have you ever considered the possiblility that sometimes physical death is a healing? The following stories tell us a side of humanity which our society shuns. It is about the time of finality which we must all face eventually. When a pet animal is gravely ill and appears to be in agony, our society graciously allows us to put it to sleep legally. In fact, it is often viewed as a kindness to the suffering animal as well as an ending to what may also mean enormous veterinary expenses. In our human society, we face quite another challenge. Perhaps the ethical aspects are based in religious beliefs? Why do we keep dying, and incurably ill people alive by artificial means? Occasionally the family intercedes on behalf of a patient and goes to court to remove someone from artificial life supports like feeding tubes or oxygen. At times, is keeping a person alive and suffering simply another way to make money off someone's misery? Here we pose more questions than answers. We want you to be the judge if dying can sometimes also be called a "HEALING."

And we invite you to contact us in the future with your honest opinions.

Chapter Eighteen

Nikko's Story

Nikko loved his uncle as if he was a father. The relationship was supposed to have been legally cemented by an adoption, but Uncle Minos fell too ill to complete the legalities in time. Instead, the acceptable next of kin was Uncle Minos' sister, who was very interested in managing Minos' financial holdings, but not all that interested in the healthcare given to the now senile man. One day Nikko received a telephone call from a concerned and furious nurse in ICU where unbeknown to Nikko, his seriously ill uncle was being housed and treated.....

In nothing short of a rage the irate nurse asked Nikko, "What kind of animals are you in your family?" Nikko was utterly shocked. After many questions and answers this is what he found out from the nurse. Uncle Minos had had a stroke and was found comatose. After two days his neighbor felt something was very wrong. When she finally saw Minos lying sprawled on the floor through a window, the neighbor called for an ambulence. Although time and time again it had been suggested to the next of kin that a home health aide be hired with responsibility of caring for Minos, this simply did not happen soon enough to avoid a tragedy.

Nikko also learned that the hospital had resuscitated his uncle five times over a one week period. In the year this occurred, that hospital charged $50,000.00 per resuscitation. Rushing to see his uncle, Nikko was desperately trying to understand why they kept bringing an incurable human

68

vegetable back to life. When he got to the hospital, the legal next of kin was not there. No one could reach her or had any idea where the sister in charge was located. She was away traveling on vacation.

Nikko pleaded with officials to stop resuscitating Uncle Minos. He was informed to "Mind his own business as he was not the accepted next of kin, and had no rights in this legal matter."

Fate stepped in and Uncle Minos did not live more than another day. In this sad and expensive situation, was death a healing for Uncle Minos? Should his sister have left instructions on where to be reached?

Chapter Nineteen

Mickey

Mickey had cancer from his head to his toes. At some point it became impossible for him to remain at home because too many medical procedures were required to keep him alive. With the deepest sorrow a family could feel, he was taken to a hospital that was considered humane to those who were terminally ill. This was before we had hospices.

Papers were filled out on his behalf asking that nothing artificial be done to prolong his life. With Mickey's last breath he requested this and believed, along with his family, that his wishes would be honored. One day his wife came in to a scene that has remained to torture her for the rest of her own life. She found them holding Mickey in an upright position on the hospital bed while removing fluid from his lungs with a massive needle. Mickey was no longer able to speak at this time.

His spine had totally disintegrated from the cancer and he had been prone and a quadraplegic for the last nine months of his life. The act of sitting had been renounced nine months prior because it caused him unendurable pain. All the doctors, nurses, and attendants knew this. Yet the doctor was holding Mickey in a sitting position to perform surgery. The wife came in unannounced and told the doctor to gently put the dying man down. She calmly insisted they stop the procedure, which having been caught, they did. Her husband had passed out mercifully. She remained until he came to, at which time he whispered to her

"Kill me with the pillow." Since this was not an option, he then asked her to "Leave, but put the air-conditioner on super high." Again she refused.

The next day when she visited, the air-conditioner was on super high. Apparently someone had been asked by Mickey to do the dying man a favor.

By that evening he fell into a coma and died four days later. Did he commit suicide to end the suffering from the cancer as well as from the medical staff? Was the person who did actually put the air-conditioning on super high aware that this caused Mickey to contract pneumonia, which then led to his coma and death? Did the ending of his mortal pain fall under the heading of a healing?

Chapter Twenty

Love Me Enough To Let Me Go

I was contacted to pray for my two friends' dying mother. They were distraught and begging for help. When I went to see their mom, it was with a heavy heart. She had been such a wonderful mother to them. Even on the outskirts looking in, I myself had grown to love this lady. And this woman was a "lady." Such dignity and joy for life. Layla's wit, charm, and ability to entertain lavishly were things I will always cherish. Yet now, she herself had lost all desire to continue. She told me how much she had tried to beat the illness wracking her now all too thin body, and just "could not fight anymore." But her saddened children were beseeching Layla to struggle on for their sakes. It wasn't that long ago their father died. This was a messy situation filled with all the emotional crisis a truly close and loving family could endure. My role in this saga was soon to turn into an advocate for Layla's predicament.

The doctors had no hope for resolving her health. After many operations to fix a chronic heart condition, everything had failed. In addition, the operations had drained her last ounce of strength. Layla wanted to pass on and end the torture. She could not eat, walk, barely breathed, and passed out constantly from lack of blood being circulated through her withering body. She spoke to me for the last time and begged me to show her children that she just could not hold on for them any longer. I asked my friends to meet me in a neutral location away from the hospital. We spoke for many hours in

St. Patrick's Cathedral. Perhaps it was the atmosphere of this great place of worship. Or, maybe it was the timing.... but instead of praying for Layla to live, I asked them if we could instead pray for "The Right And Perfect Outcome" for Layla, the family, and all concerned.

After many hours of praying and meditation we went to visit their mother at the hospital. We were informed that during the time we had been in the cathedral, Layla had peacefully slipped away in her sleep. For the first time in years she had a smile on her face in death. The ending of pain allowed her beautiful face to smile once again. Somehow, our prayer for the right and perfect outcome seemed answered in a way that was already decided by fate anyway. Prolonging the suffering was an issue in this family. Would you have done the same thing we finally did?

A few months went by and I was again in touch with my friends after Layla's funeral. For them it had been a great learning about loving someone enough to let them go. Although they truly missed their mother and were grieving still, both of them thanked me for listening to a request made by a brave woman who had been hanging on to placate her children. They realized that there was no hope left and in begging her to continue to fight, they were hurting her all the more. Since she passed away, both my friends have dreamt of their mother smiling on them. They claim to still feel her presence and loving warmth.

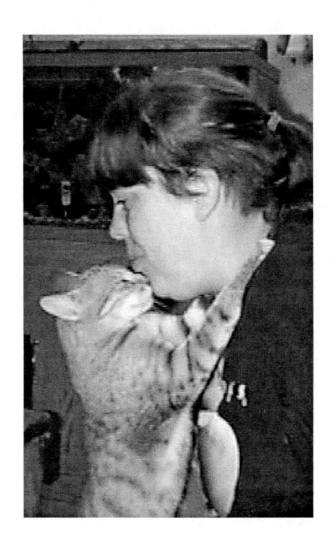

Chapter Twenty One

Our Amazing Animals

People and animals have intertwined their lives since the very beginning of our species. It hasn't stopped since then. We would like to present you with some heartwarming accounts of "Our Amazing Animals." Sometimes they play the role of life savers while they also help to heal us with their unconditional love and loyalty. Telepathy and other aspects of Extra Sensory Perception will further endear them to you. It has long been known that pets can lengthen and enhance the lives of their human owners. Of course this works both ways. A number of the stories are quite current, but most are derived out of a lifetime of compiling testimonials from the many people who have lovingly told us about their furry roommates. We begin with a personal account of how my family's pet cat "Biggie" saved Grandma Minnie's life back in the 1950's.

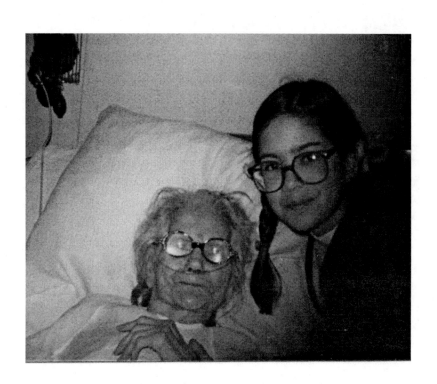

Chapter Twenty Two

Biggie Saved Grandma's Life

"Oh my God is Grandma Minnie sick!" Mom was out of her mind with concern. Our home had two floors with the bedrooms being layed out upstairs. This was very inconvenient when someone was seriously sick. My grandmother lived with us and our responsibility was to care for her in this time of need. She had pneumonia. Don't kid yourself. This was a grave, dangerous illness then. Particularly since grandma had just undergone intense radiation therapy and a radical mastectomy. (A note to you in advance. Grandma Minnie disliked cats intensely, and wanted us to dump ours. We had argued over this heated issue many times).

She was given her very first dose of anti-biotics and we were told this should help her pneumonia quite rapidly. Grandma asked us to close the door and drifted off to sleep. In the middle of the night, Biggie woke me up. She was pulling on my nightgown. At first I thought I was dreaming. Biggie kept pulling me until there was no choice but to get up and see what was going on. She led me to the door to my grandmother's bedroom. But it was left open. How could this be when we had closed it? I went in to find a horrible sight. My grandmother was choking to death. She could not talk but gasped and made gurgling sounds. Apparently Biggie hadopened the door with both paws. Don't ask how. I still cannot figure it out. She had never done this before. We called up for emergency help and the ambulance seemed to take forever. As soon as they arrived they ascertained that her throat had swelled closed. Immediately, they slit a cut into her throat and inserted a tube for her to breathe with. Then she was rushed to the hospital. Biggie was a heroine.

In those days no one knew that a person could be life and death allergic to anti-biotics. Seems like my grandmother was. Later on we were to find out that her daughter, my mother, was too. I suppose you are wondering if Biggie's act of brilliance was rewarded? My cat was a star, and couldn't have cared less about my grandmother's hateful attitude towards her. Wouldn't you know it that as soon as Grandma Minnie came back she started the same old nonsense all over again about not wanting cats. Can you imagine if we had actually given in to what this crotchety woman demanded and finally dumped our beloved pet? By rights, Grandma should have died, and it would sadly have been her own fault. Instead, she lived to be eighty-seven, ironically thanks in great part to a cat.

Chapter Twenty Three

Brittany The Feline Heroine

Brittany had a morning routine that never seemed to be altered. She would proudly prance along with her masters in the street until the children got onto their school bus, and then walk alongside her adult owner until they returned home. Then she would have breakfast while the coffee was brewing and watch T.V. with her lady owner. It was most unusual for Brittany to walk away on her own. But this is precisely what happened. Her mistress followed with great curiosity until they reached the home of a younger sister who resided two full blocks away.

Immediately, it was obvious something was very wrong. Smoke and fumes were pouring out of the windows. Without thinking Brittany's owner ran into the house to find her sister and children asleep. Their kerosene heater had been left on and it malfunctioned.

All might have died in their sleep if Brittany had not varied their morning routine. What prompted this cat to saunter away from her master and do something she had not ever done before? How did she know the house, two full blocks away, was in trouble? Brittany became a feline hero. But from what wonderful dimension did the information come in order for the cat to lead her master to the emergency?

Chapter Twenty Four

Sammy's Show of Sympathy

Sammy was my wife's cat all the way. He merely tolerated my presence. Whenever I tried to stroke him, he would fluff up his huge tail, turn his back on me, and jump up into my wife's lap. This was Sammy's way of showing that he belonged to her, and I was not as special to his royal feline-ness.

The morning my father passed away was very hard on me. I came home from the hospital and had to sit down on the couch. Then Sammy came over to me purring. "Strange behavior for the cat" I thought. Without hesitation he jumped up on my lap and sat there for two loving hours. During that time Sammy stroked me with his paws, stared into my eyes, and purred his heart out to me. My wife took in this odd sight and asked me "What the !@#@! was going on?"

To this day Sammy has not jumped back onto my lap again. As soon as I enter the room, he goes right to my wife ignoring me with his quirky cat independence (which I must admit I do love). I believe his act of sympathy, physical affection, and gentle kindness when dad died was triggered by the change in my own energy output and vibration. The look on his face when he stared deeply into my eyes was nearly human. It seemed to me that in his way Sammy was saying, "O.K. this is a really big event, and I'm here for you in your time of need."

Chapter Twenty Five

Purrrr-Therapy

For a number of years, we have used "purrrr-therapy" cats in our counseling practice. It began with a rescue kitten, an all black neutered male, named "Magick." At the time he came into our lives, we did not even want a pet. He was about to be put to sleep the following day in a kill shelter, when the lucky kittie sort of fell into our laps. It was one of the nicest things that has ever happened to us. At first he seemed terrified of everything.... and was skinny, ugly, sickly and always whining. I'm certain his mother and littermates were dead. After a few weeks he began to thrive on our love and nurturing. Magick has since blossomed into a bonafide full-blown genius. He may have the highest feline I.Q. I've ever seen. So that you can picture him his description is as follows:

* 100% black.
* Weighs 18 pounds of muscle and a bit pudgy. (More to hug).
* Very long paws with hindquarters a bit higher than his shoulders and front paws.
* Huge expressive almond shaped apple green eyes.
* Small rounded ears.
* Chatters around the clock with a larger vocabulary than most humans. ie: Right before he will open a door knob, he tells you the sounds that clearly indicates such.

Our home office door was closed and my patient was in a light trance while experiencing hypnotherapy. The first time Magick did his astounding therapy as a professional, he had silently opened the tightly closed door with both his paws and entered the room without my knowledge. He then decided to jump up onto our massage table and press his head in the crook of the arm of my hypnotized patient.

I watched in astonishment and asked the gentleman if he wanted "The loud purring to stop?" Still in trance, I was told, "Not on your life. It feels good and makes me feel safe." Then Magick instinctively began breathing in synch with the man and fell asleep in what appeared to be his own trance.

The session went extremely well, far better than our others. We made so much headway in the trauma release the man came for. At the end of the session, I gently brought him out of trance and back to this realm. Magick awoke and simply padded softly out of the room, his work done.

He has been mentoring our brightest kittens since then. At times a therapy cat will locate an injured or hurting physical part of a patient's body and purr close to the afflicted area. Other times they will simply pace their breathing with a patient and rest next to them while asleep or in a light trance themselves. Invariably it helps the sessions flow more smoothly, as well as bringing about increased progress for some people. For those who request Purrrr-Therapy, it really seems to be a healthy adjunct to their healing process.

On days when the kitties work this way, it seems that our household is more relaxed and the cats are too. Oh yes, Magick asked me to tell you that he cannot work with everyone. He has chosen not to interact with people who are addicts or child molestors. It has something to do with the altered brain waves and electro-magnetic frequency they emit.

Chapter Twenty Six

Feline Health Intuitive

"Lovey" is a Bengal female cat owned by John, an associate. John is a health professional, breeder of show cats, rescues many abandoned animals, and then carefully finds homes for them. He is also a person with a few serious health challenges himself. Lovey has become an accurate barometer for John's well being and can consistently surmise danger long in advance of an illness manifesting itself in her master. Here are some of the wonderful skills this cat has shown....

* Lovey seems to know ahead of an epileptic seizure that it will be coming on.
* She senses infection at the site before it errupts.
* Lovey gives massages to areas of pain.
* She scans her master's body for diseases and will stop at the area that is going to be manifesting trouble and purrs at it.

Here is a story related to us about Lovey's tender healing skills, from John."One day we were cuddling and Lovey decided to do her body scanning technique on me. She went all over from my legs upwards until she reached the area of my left ear. Doctor Lovey started to sniff my ear which at this time felt perfectly healthy.

Then Lovey began her purring into my ear. Because she has been so accurate in her diagnosis of past things, I decided to go for an examination. The earliest possible appointment was one week later. But two days after Lovey did her psychic scan and sniffed on my ear, I awoke with a raging pain deep inside

my head. I also had a high fever, nausea, and joint pain. It felt like that awful flu bug, and particularly afflicted was my left ear.

Well, I was too sick to go to a doctor, but prevailed upon mine to make a house call.Yes, yes, I know this is rare nowadays. But the doctor owed me a favor. She found a large pussy abcess lodged deep inside my left ear. Two days before this infection painfully emerged into the material world, my wonderful cat Lovey knew I would be ill and warned me. Luckily, I did not take the business trip that had been previously scheduled. It isn't fun to get sick away from your own home. This is how much I trust and respect "Doctor Lovey."

Chapter Twenty Seven

Our Cats Take Care of Us

This story was submitted to me by a family in Indonesia. They live on a very large farm and have many animals other than their beautiful and extremely expensive exotic looking kitties. Their cats never go outside for fear they would be eaten by predators. The home itself is comprised of 18,000 square feet of spacious elegance. For them, felines are royalty, and actually wear bejeweled collars. This story is one of love and loyalty.

The mistress of the house suffers with a recurring and chronic connective tissue disorder. When the condition flares up it has a tendency to dislocate her bones.Needless to say, this is quite painful. In fact, it has been so severe that it forced her in one particularly fierce attack to become bedridden.

Although the cats have their own wing of this immense home, they all crowded onto their owner's super king sized bed. Then each one picked an area the woman was afflicted in, and began to lick her. All six cats continued massaging her around the clock and would only leave to eat, drink and go potty. They would immediately return to do their licking routines on their mistress. According to this regal lady, they instinctively knew exactly where each bone was not aligned in the proper place. Her own physician did not know this information without the use of X-Rays.

Chapter Twenty Eight

Nadia's Gift For Healing

Nadia felt something was just not right. At age seven this child was a very sensitive girl. She desperately walked all around the rented bungalow her family had leased for the summer up in the mountains. Nadia searched for whatever it was that was calling to her without a sound. Somehow the young girl could feel how much a baby kitten was suffering, although it made not a peep. Finally, Nadia cautiously moved the branches of a bush and there lay the silent, dying cat.

"Mommy, Mommy" she shouted. "Hurry." This is how Nadia the adult recalled the first time she could simply sense an injured animal needed help. It initiated a profound relationship between her and nature. Later on in life as a medical health intuitive, clairvoyant, and ultimately a doctor, she would transfer this unusual gift over to humans as well.

The kitten had to be picked up gently and brought to their small country kitchen as quickly as possible. It was completely dehydrated and too young to be without its mother's milk. In addition, there was a leech deeply imbedded in its right shoulder sucking the very life from the baby. Nadia assisted her mother immediately and without question. It was as if they had done this many times before.

They quickly took an eye dropper and gave it water. It did not struggle. In fact, the kitten allowed them quietly to cut open her gaping infected wound and remove the bloodsucker. They poured sulfur powder straight onto and into the open hole which went all the way down to the female kitten's shoulder bone. How brave the baby was. They both felt she knew they were trying to save it from death.

After they did their best to clean her up, Nadia's mother got new white sewing thread and deftly sewed the wound closed. More sulfur went on and then a clean bandage was wrapped around the baby to keep it safe from further injury to the damaged shoulder.

That day they were to eat chicken soup, vegetables, and boiled chicken. It was already on the stove, so they tried to feed the kitten. No deal. The baby could not take food at all. So they pureed the vegetables and chicken in the broth and fed it through the eye dropper for a full week around the clock. This worked. The kitten began to make sounds and purr softly. What a wonderful feeling Nadia had about saving the kitten's life. It never even dawned on her that she was distinctly different from other children.

Over the years many animals benefitted from Nadia's ability to sense injury, disease and impending illness in this remarkable manner. She could be in a room with complete strangers and know their medical history. It was uncanny. When Nadia was a teenager she intentionally and completely shut down this gift. It caused her to be viewed as a weird kid which she found very embarrassing. Someone had even told her that she "Could and should be put away in an asylum for crazy people because she was so different." Being a teenager, Nadia flew with the crowd and just wanted to fit in. This went on until her twenty-first birthday. Then, and without conscious intent, the gift returned full blast! Nadia went into shock believing she would be put away with the crazy people. The more she tried not to be psychic, the more psychic she became.

It got so intense that she could read minds and even repeat back the thoughts people had right in front of them. In fear and confusion, she finally met up with someone she liked and respected enough to share her unnerving experience with verbally.

Luckily for her and all those people and animals she has since been an instrument of healing for, Nadia was given sage advice. "No, you are not crazy" the wise friend kindly said. "Yes, you are extremely psychic and should be trained properly." The path of a shaman was very exciting and laborious, holding out for the young woman the study of botanicals and alternative medical modalities. Many years went into perfecting the art of her reading auras and the significance of colors surrounding a life form. Yet this was not enough for such a gifted one. Nadia wanted to be a medical doctor. Doctor Nadia would have the respect of John Q. Public and remain quiet for a while as a "closet shaman."

By the time she graduated as a physician, Nadia had reached the age of fifty. To some fifty is old. For her it was the prime of her life. Remember that this woman used herbs, meditation, and concoctions from many cultures. She had also mastered acupuncture. Instead of utilizing a lot of needles, Nadia used as few as possible and instinctively knew where they could be best placed in her patients. In fact, she told me one of the reasons for her extremely youthful face. She used the needles to bring about cosmetic surgery. I am not surprised. The woman does not seem to appear thirty-five, let alone fifty.

Her roster of patients is immensely helped by Nadia the doctor. What many of her traditional clientele do not realize is that these very same accurate and competent diagnostic skills are being enhanced dramatically by the psychic ability she had been given. Ironically, it was this exact gift that tortured Nadia when as a teenager she feared being ostracized for being an intuitive and sensitive. What a blessing for me that she calls me "friend." What a blessing for her patients that she chose not to throw the talent away permanently.

Chapter Twenty Nine

A Father Saves His Daughter's Life

This story was sent in by a man living in New York City. He is still not clear about all the unusual circumstances, and yet they led him to save his own daughter's life.

"I was coming home from work on the subway when for no reason that makes any sense my feet decided to take a completely different route to walk home from the train station. It was already dark on a gloomy winter evening. I felt hungry and just wanted to throw off my shoes, eat some dinner, watch television and go to sleep. Why did I choose to take a new way home?

As I walked briskly, there was the realization that I faintly heard muffled sounds. In New York City, sounds are frequently loud, very common, and rarely listened to. But something drew me closer to these particular noises. Then I heard what seemed to be a loud scream.... and instead of running away, I rushed to where the ruckus was coming from.

Normally, I am not a fighter, nor am I particularly brave. My short height of five feet four inches did not call for many athletic sports either. Yet, I found myself grabbing a tall man's collar attached to his leather jacket and pulling him off a young girl. He was attacking the youngster while attempting to rape her. They were in a hidden away alley. There is no way to explain my new found physical strength at the time

because it was as if I had become super human. Over and over I punched the assailant, not even feeling that I broke two of my own fingers in the act. He ran away for his life, and if it wasn't for the young girl, I would have chased him down and possibly killed him.

Still not seeing the girl's face I asked her how she felt? Her trembling answer was "Daddy, is that you?"

Although this monstrosity of a pervert was able to escape me, he did not escape the two plain clothes officers who heard the scuffle and gave chase. A higher wisdom forced me to take a totally strange route home that particular night. I shudder to think what would have happened if instead I used the normal route."

Chapter Thirty

A Laboratory Experiment In Telepathy

We are not advocating that you try this interesting experiment sent to us by a parapsychologist. But the results are repeatable and quite baffling. It is best done with from four to ten people. If these numbers aren't practical, as few as three will do.

Our experiment begins with whoever volunteers first to be blindfolded. Then cotton is put into the ears to deaden sound. All participants are not to wear shoes in order to further quieten any noises. Make sure the blindfolds are on very securely as it is integral to this experiment that the people really NOT be able to see or hear.

Put the blindfolded person in the middle of the participants. Each of the seeing people takes a turn doing the following:

Tap the blindfolded person on the shoulder and move away. Go to another place and again tap the blindfolded person on the wrist. Go to another place and tap the blindfolded person on the head. Continue doing this until the person begins to ward off the contacts through mental vision. Usually it takes most people about three to four minutes for their psychic visual skills to kick in.

The blindfolded people go through a range of emotions. First it is surprise. Then annoyance. We find most become really angry. From anger, the people almost always begin to know where the tapper is before being touched and wards off the contact. Please remember "NOT" to hit anyone hard. This is about learning how we can see with another sensibility than our eyes or ears.

Let each person take their turn being blindfolded and tapped. It almost never fails to be an exciting and immensely educational event. When we did it for the first time, it startled me at how angry and vulnerable I felt at the onset. Although we timed everyone precisely three minutes apiece, for most it really felt like an eternity. Once the angry phase passed and I could see/feel exactly where the tapping was coming from with my third eye senses, I felt an elation come over me. Actually, we all became euphoric with a new knowledge of power. It was one of the most exciting experiments we've ever participated in, and we did it with six people. Learn and enjoy! Our group wonders just how ancient this rite might truly be?

Chapter Thirty One

Did You See That Apparition Too?

What is bi-location? We have read about religious masters being able to appear in more than one place at a time. For the family that sent in this story, their loved one did the same thing upon his demise.

Each testimony has been sworn to by those who have claimed to see the deceased. He allegedly appeared to a relative in a hospital, approximately 50 miles away. Then he was also seen in another state by two of his friends and co-workers who were driving home after a musical performance. Yet he was physically with his brother who attended the comatose man in person at the hospice where he actually died. Each person(s) saw him the same night he passed away, but in totally different and far off locations. Finally, the man who died was a quadraplegic. His doctor and a nurse were with him too.

The relative in the distant hospital was herself gravely ill. They had been arch enemies in life. The woman had been hospitalized for the last two months and not expected to live from complications of advanced diabetes. In the middle of the night while heavily sedated for heart problems, she was awakened by a voice. It said to her that the man was now dead, the exact time he died, and showed her a picture of him. In the picture he was illuminated in a million watts of irridescent light. He was laid out on a slab in the middle of

an auditorium. Her forgiveness was requested. She awoke from the drugged state and began screaming for help. Over and over she kept saying "Her son-in-law had died. Give me something to draw what I have seen."

The hysterical woman was placated by a nurse, given the pad and pencil, and drew what she saw plus what had been told to her. And with the precise accuracy of the doctor who was attending the man who just died, the exact time of death was notated by her which coincided with what the attending physician officially declared was the moment of death for her son-in-law.

Because this woman was seriously ill, her own family chose not to tell her that her son-in-law was also dying. There was no way she could have known at a conscious level that he passed away at the exact time she had her phenomenal middle of the night visitation.

The two musicians were driving home from a club they had worked in that same evening. It was very late and neither of them drink or do drugs. In fact, they are extremely conservative older men. At the same time the man died in the far off hospice, they were in a distant state. Suddenly, his face and torso appeared in their car. It was illuminated from his shoulders up. In their mutual language of Spanish, both men swear to the same statement. The dying man told them "I was indeed your friend. I have just died and came to say goodbye. Please do not be afraid. I love you." Then their car began to rock and shake as if they were in the middle of a violent storm. They were terrified, shocked, and in a state of disbelief at what they both agreed was their dear friend's farewell visit. Upon arriving home they both had messages saying he had died while they saw his apparition in their car.

When I began asking people for stories of this nature, the family offered up their astonishing tale. They have sworn that all of the viewings have been corroborated and attested to. Of the people involved, I received seven testimonials that every word is the truth. The gentleman who passed away was not religious at all. In life he had a very strong and vivacious personality. According to all the medical people I have interviewed who attended him, he fought to live against medically impossible circumstances. His friends were many. And so were his enemies. All agreed he was a bigger than life type of man. No one seemed bland about their personal feelings for him one way or another. He had struggled for an inordinate length of time to survive this terminal illness. In death, his energy had such a forcefulness to it that these people claim he was able to show and communicate himself in multiple locations all at the same time. The synchronicities of this story are both baffling and intriguing. No one has ever come up with any solid explanations for how this phenomena of bi-location could occur.

Chapter Thirty Two

Visits From Spirit

The following story comes to us from a Jewish family. When they were sitting Shiva for their deceased mother, something happened that was witnessed by the newly buried lady's friends and family. (Sitting Shiva is a custom which has the loved ones sitting on wooden boxes to show respect for a deceased person). It is written in the first person by one of her daughters.

"Once the horror of mommy's funeral was over with, we returned home to my brother's apartment to sit Shiva. Many people came over with food which is part of the custom. Our mirrors were covered, as is traditional, so that respect is shown the deceased. I cannot say how many were there when mom appeared. People had been walking in and out all day long. Perhaps at the moment we all saw her, there were twenty people jammed into my brother's tiny living room.

I sat on a wooden box while friends were talking to me. I looked up because it seemed a light was just turned on. To my teared up eyes I caught a glimpse of my mother smiling at me. It had been a nasty time without much sleep. So I rubbed my eyes. But she was still smiling at me. Then my young son pulled my hand and said "Grandma is here mom, don't be sad." I asked if she was visible to him and he said "Of course, can't you see her?" Then he pointed to exactly where I saw the light and my mother's image. A friend who had adored my mom looked over at where my son pointed to and gasped out loud. Again, another person had seen her. This went on until

a total of five people said they saw her where I could see her. Then.... nothing.

I like to joke that we were a bit crazy, but this is unrealistic. How could five separate people all have seen her in one location after we had buried my mother's body that very same day in a cemetery? Even after my brother said he saw our mother, my brother still does not believe it. I do, and so does my son. My friend, and our rabbi who attended her at the end do too."

Chapter Thirty Three

The Visit From Hell

When we hear from scientists that only a very small percent of our brain is being used, the following story seems to magnify these thoughts. Is there a universal mind somewhere out there that brings people together in a manner that we always have to question? How is it possible for people in distinct and far flung locations to have the identical dream at the exact same time? The story you are about to read discusses this phenomenon.

Aiyesha and her mother Fatima were brutalized by Harmud. Not only was it legal in their homeland for a man to beat his wife and incest his daughters, but it was applauded by other men. For the sake of protecting these women who now live in another country, we shall not indicate which land they were born in. Somehow, God had gotten tangled up in the customs, which according to these people made it perfectly all right to behave this way. They were still deeply indoctrinated themselves. Both women had been circumcised as children, which was also the accepted but loathed custom. It was forbidden that a female should enjoy having sex. Anyway, this was the rationale told to me. Both women remained fearful of repercussions although they now lived in a place that legally allowed women to own property and re-marry if they became widowed. Fatima made me understand that she preferred to die single and widowed. Aiyesha too did not wish to marry anyone, although she was certainly a very physically beautiful and highly intelligent young woman.

When they had their mutual dream about Harmud, it was while both were asleep in two different locations. Harmud had died at fifty-nine from a massive coronary thrombosis.

The lack of phones and communications in their homeland makes this even more bizarre, since neither woman learned about the other's dream until some time had passed after Harmud's death. They were at a family wedding when Aiyesha saw her mother. Fatima was longing to converse privately with her daughter. Finally, they were alone and away from family prying ears and wagging tongues. The mother told Aiyesha she had a grotesque nightmare visitation from Harmud after he died.

He appeared on a three legged stool. The room he was in seemed to be a dungeon, and its atmosphere was terrible. The air was thick, murky, green and slimy. Harmud was unable to speak because his tongue had been cut out. Both hands were tied behind his back with barbed wire, so movement would hurt him. His eyes bulged out of his head, as if an invisible vice was choking his brains. Harmud was in mortal agony, but definitely not on earth. He could speak, but only telepathically with his tormented eyes.

The story he mentally told was about his punishment for all the torture he had foisted upon them. Upon being sent to hell he realized that he always did have a choice. The custom of wife beating and incesting female children was not followed by all men. He chose this behavior and now had to pay. When his spiritual sentence was to be finished, Harmud told Fatima that he would again visit and show her he was free. By the time these words were said to Aiyesha, both women were literally hysterical because Aiyesha had suffered through the identical dream the same night Fatima dreamt it.

Seven years later they were once more visited by Harmud in a dream on the same night. Both women slept in two different

locations. Harmud showed them that he had been set free for his spiritual crimes against his family.

An interesting aspect to all this abuse is that both Fatima and Aiyesha were filled with pain to learn about his severe punishment. Neither woman claimed to have felt pleasure or revenge from Harmud's visible torment in hell.

Chapter Thirty Four

Finding Lost Things With The Help of Saint Anthony

This happy and very light hearted account of finding a precious object that had been lost was recounted to us by Eduardo. Eddy had long been an atheist. In fact he was quite proud of his intellect and mental-ness. The idea of the Catholic Saint Anthony being a friend to those who have lost things was about number one million on Eduardo's belief list.

Many years ago, Eduardo's father was losing his ability to walk from a fatal disease. Eddy had just been born. As a gesture of love, his father bought one last gift for the baby he would never see grow up. He purchased a very expensive and well made snub nosed baby scissor. It meant the world to Eddy and his mother, and was held in a cherished position until it was somehow lost outside of their home while visiting a relative in another city.

Years later when Eduardo was nine they moved. All brown paper supermarket bags were discarded prior to this move.

One Sunday they went to a feast day held in Greenwich Village for Saint Anthony. There were delicious ethnic foods, beautiful ceremonies, assorted stands, and lots of free fun. A relic was reverently brought out for the worshippers to see which was purportedly from the famous Saint Anthony himself. And the story of how he helps those to find and reclaim that which has been lost was re-told for the zillionth time.

When Eddy and his mom returned home from the festivities, they had things they wished to store away in a brown supermarket bag which was housed in the pantry. As his mother opened their pantry door, the following event happened. First they heard a man sweetly giggle. Then straight up in the air flew the lost baby scissor.

It was catapulted with great force and hit the ceiling before it fell into Eduardo's waiting hands. In disbelief and happy amazement they had been reunited with the precious gift a dying man had lovingly bought for his baby boy.

According to Eduardo and his mother, the only brown paper bags they had in this pantry closet "Had been acquired in the past few months from grocery shopping." They said that "The sound of light-hearted laughter they heard was supposed to have been the manner in which Saint Anthony returns lost objects. It is customary for a sweet giggle to accompany the find." Eduardo will be the first person to admit his gift was returned to them by Saint Anthony's benevolence. And yes, Eduardo is still rigidly a devout atheist.

Chapter Thirty Five

When Objects Move by Themselves....
(We bought a Haunted House)

Our next story was submitted by a family of two doctors and one engineer. Living together in an exceptionally scientifically oriented home and logical life style, these three people have experienced many unusual happenings since moving into their older house. From the first day until present, odd and inexplicable phenomena have been happening. Initially, the feeling was one of surprises, disbelief, and queasy fear. Now it seems that whatever is going on the damage and pranks have simmered down to the point where everyone is able to tolerate and accept the others' presence in peace and quiet.

Absolutely not one thing went right from the beginning. The sellers lied on as much as they could get away with, while the old crafty man who had been the owner even paid off the realtors and inspector to make the sale go through.

By the time the family who bought this home realized their own move-in day, the old man who sold them his "house of lies" had beaten our trio out of a fortune of money. He even became a squatter for three months, refusing to so much as pay a dime in rent to the new buyers, until threatened with legal eviction proceedings. Even then, the old man left the

118

new buyers seventeen years worth of his garbage to have to get rid of.

On the first day they had a flood from the alleged "perfect plumbing system." While mopping up the deluge caused by clogged pipes, the engineer father thought to ask where the papers were that made them the new owners? Apparently after putting them down on the kitchen counter, they disappeared. Neither his wife nor his son had a clue as to where they were either. After a long and arduous search, they found the documents lying in disarray upstairs in a bathroom.

Since they were the only ones at home, and all had seen them being placed on the kitchen counter, finding them upstairs made no sense. Anyway, grateful to have found them, the valuable papers were put away in a folder in their filing cabinet.

The mother and son, which we will name Iriana and Solomon, were carrying on a conversation in their livingroom while papers pertaining to the repair on the faulty plumbing were lying in front of them. Both people attest to the fact that the papers rose up in mid-air while there was absolutely not a breeze in the house. They remained floating for a while and then fell down to the floor in a sloppy heap.

They had moved in with two pet dogs. Since there was painting and remodeling work going on, the doors were closed to all the rooms in order to protect the animals from getting into the paint. No matter how many times the doors were tightly closed, they mysteriously became opened without human intervention. This happened so often the family stopped counting. Just as soon as a door was closed is how fast it got reopened. And this even occurred while they were viewing it.

Frequently, there would be the feeling that a certain area got chilly or just plain cold. Even though they lived in a warm climate, a chill would come right before an event of the paranormal began to transpire. It did not happen 100% of the time. Finally, the family began charting these scary events to keep a written record.

One day both phone lines were in use for their computers when the doorbell rang. Outside stood the police. Upon asking why they were there, the policeman said, "They had been called to come to their home for an emergency."

Iriana showed the police that both computers were utilizing her two phone lines and that she was still logged on. Nonetheless, they showed her the record of having been called. The following week it happened all over again. This time Solomon was alone at home using one phone line for a computer and the other for a long distance call. Yet the police claimed his phone number had called them with an emergency at exactly the same time both his telephones were in use.

About two months after they moved in, notes began to be left by the front door. They were signed by the old man who had sold them the house. They compared his signatures to the official papers he had signed at their closing. Upon doing an investigation, they discovered that he had died in a fire the month before. Wanting to be careful and scientific, the family went to a professional graphologist. The signatures on the notes were the same as the signatures on the closing papers.

About four months after they moved in one of their daughters brought over her three cats for the family to care for while she went on vacation. The entire time the cats were there all three ran after things that were not visible to the human eye. Every time it happened, their tails would become super thick from fear looking like a fox's tail, and then they would give chase to something(s) invisible. Yet, the kitties could see what it was. Each time this happened, there would be a chill in the room.

One day they decided to invite over a researcher and parapsychologist. It had been six long and testing months of odysseys without logical explanations. The rapidly mounting number of weird events forced the family to seek help. It was suggested to try Feng Shui. This is an ancient oriental art of smoothing out our environ-ment, and is somewhat based in the exorcism of nasty entities. At first, our three scientists balked. But then after yet another harrowing siege, they finally acquiesced.

Little eight sided beveled mirrors were put up at every entrance and exit. All toilet seats were to be closed when not in use. The rationale behind this is that entities would not enjoy seeing themselves when they arrive or exit by the reflection in the mirrors. The toilet gets rid of waste and human garbage, so by closing the lids, they were drawing a line of protection. Instead of getting better, things got dramatically worse. It was as if something became terribly jostled in the effort to rid this old house of its hauntings. New tactics were required with the nasty turn of events.

A Native American shaman was brought in and he walked through 100% of the house, including the closets, with burning sage. This is a cleansing custom that has been used for millennia. Not only did things not improve, but it became so bad that three pictures fell off the walls. They were hung with engineering precison by the father. After he (Santo) inspected the walls where the pictures had fallen off, there were gaping holes as if something had ripped them apart with a sledge hammer. Life in this house had become so stressful that they were actually considering throwing in the towel, selling it and moving on.

One more attempt was made to get rid of whatever did not want them living there. A group of Nigerian drummers reputed to have incredible spiritual gifts were asked to help them. The appointment was made for the drumming and preparations were expected of the three owners.

First they had to wash all the floors with flower petals. They were asked to wear only white attire and fast for a day in advance of the ceremony. Since all the trouble had begun with the vicious old man who had sold them the house.... they were instructed to pray for his dead soul. Candles of assorted colors including white were to be lit in every corner of the home to light the way for the spirits back to wherever they were supposed to be living. At no time was anger or meanness a part of this ritual. It was based in love and respect for the alleged spirit(s) who were suffering and earthbound in this old house. With all the preparations made, the family eagerly awaited the Nigerian drummers and their age old wisdoms in such matters.

The five older men arrived with great dignity carrying their sacred drums and wearing exquisite beads. All were dressed in white. They themselves smelled like flowers fresh picked from a garden. With them arrived an incredible sense of serenity and power. Each one as an individual was a bit bigger than life. But together they were very striking in an ancient and ritualistic aura. Well, no matter what happens, our three friends were giving this house a wonderful chance at being cleansed by these experienced professional exorcists.

What occurred next in time sequence of events was beautiful and profound. Our homeowners were prepared for anything at this point. A slow and complicated rhythm began the ritual....

These five men certainly could play the drums with finesse. They sang first in unison and then in harmony. Every note was carefully chosen and enunciated with great precision.

Although they were chanting in a language that was not familiar to our three supplicants, they did seem to understand the soulful meaning anyway. It was invoking some kind of power to come and bring solace.

As the tempo picked up, so did a feeling of energy and whirling around them. They became encapsulated in that old familiar chill that would precede a visitation. And a visitation they certainly did have. With the chill came an apparition of the old man who had made their lives miserable with his lies and deceit. He was asking their forgiveness and.... was actually crying and begging for it. To the drummers this was "old hat" and nothing seemed to surprise or shock them. For the family it was very moving. The old man further let them know he did not want to move out of the house. In other words, he was asking to continue to live there with them. Now the lead drummer got verbally involved and spoke in a tongue not familiar to the family. It was obvious that the spirit was being given instructions to leave and go away. Where, they could not make out. After a few moments the air filled with electric static vibrations. Both the apparition and chill then disappeared.

Since performing the African ceremony, there have been no more nasty events. The chills have stopped. Papers do not disappear or float in the air by themselves. The one overt remnant they cannot explain is when their daughter's cats come to visit and they chase after invisible spooks.

The cats still go totally nuts with fat tails, ears back and growl at something upsetting that the homeowners cannot see. Then they dash after whatever it is and meow or snarl with great intensity. The family does feel much more at peace in the old house. They have decided to remain and further remodel the place. None of them wish to talk with anyone about what happened. They would simply like to forget and move on.

Chapter Thirty Six

Beware Of Psychic Mis-information And Frauds

For all the genuine events of a paranormal nature that "can" be attested to, this is still a very gray and hotly debated area. It is so easy for naive and trusting people to be taken advantage of when they are dealing with some intuitives.

Of course charlatans abound in all areas of life, including the business world. Whenever dealing with those who claim "They can give you a message from a dead loved one, or make you rich if you hand them "X" amount of money to pray for you" the door is often left open for mis-information and frauds. Most certainly, there are genuine intuitives. Just take your information with a grain of salt and use your own common sense in handing over your life's decisions to another's will.

The following story is a classic example of what to be careful of. Because the intuitive involved had been extraordinarily accurate on many occasions, it made the situation we are about to discuss all the more heartbreaking. He destroyed a fifteen year friendship which almost killed the woman who contributed this account to us.

We shall call the woman Lynette. Her long friendship with the intuitive, Roger and his wife Schary, had been one of lasting and loving generosity. Roger was brilliant, a genius in everything he touched, and as psychic as could be. His predictions were downright uncanny in their accuracy. When Lynette had a life problem she'd go to him for counsel.

Lynette's family was undergoing severe crisis. Her young husband had just died, her mother was gravely ill, and death seemed to surround the woman at every turn. Not knowing where else to seek help, she called Roger for a psychic reading. His information was absolutely shattering for Lynette's ears. Roger told her that "Within three more months your mother and grandmother will die." He then described their deaths graphically. This on top of her husband's recent passing was more than she could bear. Lynette fell into an even deeper depression, lost her job, and had a serious breakdown which required intense psychological counseling. Unbeknown to her at the time was the fact that Roger and Schary were going through an ugly divorce.

Three months came and went. Another three months came and went. Lynette's mother and grandmother were still alive. So the distraught woman called Roger. He was never again available to her to be spoken with. Lynette's mother lived another five years and her grandmother another three. The horrible prediction never came true. Lynette went through grief and mental suffering prematurely. And.... a deep friendship was ripped asunder. Is there a moral to this story?

Chapter Thirty Seven

The Dream That Saved Lives

Our next account comes from a person who herself works with the police when a murder cannot be solved, or a body is not present for judicial scrutiny. She is a housewife and student, very motherly and humble, and is the first person who will tell you that "Psychic information can be very on target, or totally or partially erroneous." We will call her Nayla and her friend, Irma.

Nayla was to drive to visit Irma who lived in another state. The day before the visit, Irma called up and urgently told her friend about a vivid dream she just had. In the dream Nayla was driving over a bridge and the car's brakes failed. Nayla lost control of the car, careered into a deep body of water and drowned together with her young son who was also to come for this visit. Needless to say, Nayla cancelled her road trip to Irma and took the car in for an inspection. She had just paid them to install completely new brakes the week before and was still under warranty. Irma was never told any of this information before she had the dream.

While driving to the gas station that had done the auto work, Nayla's braking system flat out failed. Fortunately, it happened a few blocks away from the repair shop she was trying to get to. She threw the gear shift into neutral praying it would slow the car. Screaming to her son to "Hit the floor" the terrified woman continued on in first gear until the

disabled car went through a red light and finally bounced off a bumper in the garage she was headed towards in the first place. Nayla was definitely not in a good mood.

The manager rushed out to see what the noise was all about and found Nayla livid with rage at the inept and life threatening work they had done on her car.

After relieving herself of the pent up fear and anger, she apologized for her barrage of shouting. In the meantime, a police car pulled up and started writing her a ticket for going through the red light. Such a commotion over brakes. The policeman knew her because she was working in his precinct at the time on a rather difficult child kidnapping case which sadly ended up becoming a homocide. The car repair shop manager gallantly paid for the traffic violation ticket. The owner of the gas station had them fix the brakes, plus give her a free tune-up. All subsequent work was completed and inspected twice. First, by the mechanic doing the work, and second by the policeman who issued her the ticket.

Irma garnered a direct hit as far as parapsychological warning messages were concerned. Both she and Nayla have shared this story with many as an example of being on target with precognitive specific information. Oh yes, in order to travel by automobile from Nayla's home to Irma's there is a major bridge to cross over spanning a very deep river.

130

Chapter Thirty Eight

World War Two Psychic Drama

Every once in a while we find a story that stands out in the middle of many dramatic and worthy accounts of the paranormal. What follows is almost too difficult to comprehend. The family that shared it with us is long dead. They suffered at the hands of the Nazis beyond belief. Yet this story should be told again to younger generations so the astonishing events involved are not lost in time.

The young German couple found themselves so much in love they decided to become engaged. Times in Europe were once more in great turmoil. But the fated lovers felt they would be safe. Their families approved of this marriage. Both of them were highly educated, spoke four languages each, and had hopes to live a good life together. He was already a medical doctor. She, a nurse. In the midst of their love the unspeakable horror began.

One by one, people were taken away to the death camps. Both Herman and Zelda lost 100% of their loved ones. He was dragged to a different death house than she. Their lives were ended for each other by a finality of events that rocked the entire world, bringing it into a conflict called "World War Two." Only after an eternity was the war ended.

Both Herman and Zelda had been tortured, enslaved, starved, and left for dead. Their survival is one that defies all rational and logical explanation. Yet they both lived. Herman was rescued in terrible health.

He spent years looking for people while living in Hungary. Zelda was rescued weighing 48 pounds on what had once been a five foot ten inch frame, lying nude in the snow while the Germans shot the last of the prisoners. How come the many bullets meant for her did not make contact? Zelda vaguely recalled that a strong soldier lifted her frozen body of flesh-less bones from the red coffin of snow.

One year later she left the hospital without many of her teeth. Eight of her fingers were gone. The complete loss of her frostbitten toes was the worst part of it all, even worse than the tuberculosis that plagued her lungs. Zelda searched in utter despair for anyone who might once have been a familiar living face.

While she was living in Rumania and Herman in Hungary, each believed the other to have died horrible deaths along with all the rest of their family. Displaced, crippled, mutilated and fed up, Zelda went to a gypsy fortune teller.

This is the story exactly as it was told to me. "The fortune teller was young, very elegant, and so pretty. She had a dimple in her chin and a twinkle in her eyes. I could not take my own eyes off her. Once, I too was very pretty. She told me I had to go to a specific street in a particular town in Hungary. There I would find Herman. He was engaged to be married and I had to hurry. The beautiful gypsy refused to be paid.

I had no money, no food, no family and no more courage. Why should I believe a total stranger who was not particularly interested in me? What could I gain from pushing myself to go to Hungary? Rumania was certainly not offering me any solace. Why should Hungary?

I went to Hungary, and even to the town that the gypsy fortune teller instructed me to visit. In a storm, I visited the street she advised. All I found was an old building with apartments. Inside were people, and I was again freezing cold and insufficiently dressed. Knocking on the door it was answered by a young woman who asked me what I wanted. Did I even know? But it was so cold I inquired if there was an apartment available, or at least a room to rent? She let me in.

Her mother owned the small apartment building and actually did have a room to rent me. Did I have the money to pay in advance? In tears I explained that I was broke and if she allowed me to clean for them I would be grateful. She looked at my finger-less hands and said "No." Then a man came into the room. I stared at him long and hard. He appeared slightly familiar. But this person was in a hurry so I could not really get a good look at his face. I went to the door to leave but had difficulty with only two fingers in opening it. The man did this for me. I did not even bother to say thank you.

Now in the freezing cold street it seemed as if my empty life was almost back in the despised concentration camp. I asked this man if he knew a cheap place that might rent me a room if I cleaned for them. With a rasping voice that choked from years of sorrow, Herman answered me."

Zelda and Herman were able to come to The United States. They lived a life together that surpasses what most people would term "successful." Their three children are famous entrepreneurs. These people were the closest family I have ever met.

Writing this story has been very difficult. It brings to mind how our species can turn into the worst of the bad. What ever brought Zelda to go to the fortune teller in Rumania is the best of the good. That the pretty gypsy had a direct hit is not the only portion of this amazing saga that inspires. But that

Zelda, in dire poverty and still so ill from her years of torture even thought to follow the advice is an enigma.

We see people who succumb to small problems and create a life of being whining professional victims. Here we have true victims who have miraculously created lives of success.

Chapter Thirty Nine

Archeology And The Paranormal

This is one of those "smiling" stories. It has not only brought substantial fame to the person who is allowing me to write it for him, but has pleasantly altered the archeologist's life as well.

Being an archeologist is a life filled with hard work. The glamour is rare and comes only with the important finds. Mostly, you are bent over and gently and diligently seeking artifacts, inscriptions, and buried things. The gentleman who tells us his account of the paranormal had worked in this field successfully for two decades. His back was starting to bother him enough to think about another way to earn a living. Climbing, bending over for hours on end in uncomfortable postions, and dealing with the elements had all exacted their price. Even the snake bites and scorpions had done bodily damage over the years. Not to be left out are his badly broken wrist, many sprains, and a fractured ankle that had been earned in twenty years of excavating the past. He did make a point of asking me to mention that "In no way am I trying to talk anyone out of becoming an archeologist."

He (Armand) and a carefully selected group of talents were combing through an ancient find in the middle east. Truly this was one of the glamour spots. It dated back to at least 3300 years ago. Armand had experienced many dreams about this archeological site and what he would find there. The night-

136

time vivid escapades began as a child. He would be on a dig and uncover a buried body of an adult male. This man was attired in clothing that was fairly well preserved. You could see the once bright colors on the delicate exquisitely woven cloth.

His hair was almost intact and resembled Armand's own mane of thick black hair. Golden bracelets, rings, and even a heavy set of pierced earrings adorned the frequently dreamt of corpse.

Designs on the jewelry were intricate, stunning, and well memorized by Armand's many repeated identical dreams. It was actually a beautiful experience that always seemed to end the same way. He would awake with the feeling of actually having discovered the man's grave, and then dig him up. The man was Armand in another life. Of this, he was absolutely certain.

But now after many years and more digs than he could count, it almost seemed as if he had made up this entire account with his vivid imagination. The archeologists broke for lunch, but Armand wasn't hungry. He continued searching for whatever artifacts the far off elusive past would allow them to encounter. Sometimes when luck was on their side, an ancient excavation would vomit up spectacular evidence. Today was just such a day!

Wandering around, Armand noticed a familiarity about what he saw and touched. It was a trance-like feeling, as if he had been there before. Yet this deja vu experience would not let go of him. The more he looked around, the more he felt familiar with what he found. A mental voice led him to follow deeper and deeper into the ground. He moved earth and stones with growing excitement. The more he uncovered, the more he felt he was really on to something spectacular. Armand could actually hear his own heart skip beats. Whatever he was destined to find, it surely was taking a long time in coming. Not once did he even think to call for help. This was totally irregular and not to their professional standards at all for safety.

Yet he was compelled on to dig and move heavy rocks. Suddenly, in the near darkness of the deepening earth, Armand saw something shiny. He nearly passed out. There lay a piece of gold. What was it?

Upon closer examination, it became clear that this was an earring. Whatever was spurring him on to work alone had him so excited he could not stop. The earring seemed very familiar in design. This is when Armand realized that the dig he was on today was different than anything he'd ever participated in before. It was the exact design he had dreamt of so many times as a youngster.

Feeling his heart ready to burst open, Armand decided he was ready to call in his co-workers. With everyone present, he began to tell them precisely what they were about to dig up. Enough credible witnesses were present to make this archeological dig evidenced beyond reproach.

Object after object was found in the locations Armand instructed his co-workers to explore. After a while, they did not even think it odd that he could tell them where to find things. The entire experience became surreal. The surreal became perfectly normal. All worked feverishly and at a level of expertise they themselves never expected to live to see happen in their careers. By the time every last artifact had been excavated from the crypt, they realized that this had been a generous gift to them, perhaps never to be surpassed for the rest of their lives as archeologists.

Years later Armand retold this adventure to a group of people who were studying with him. I was one of these students. He had long ago decided to retire from archeology and become a businessman and trainer in a totally different field of endeavor.

Still fairly young, and vitally interested and interesting, Armand made the best of all lecturers. His ability to bring past, present, and future into the learning experience was a skill used by the wisest of teachers. This was only matched by his brilliant humor and humble nature. How many people do you know who believe they have actually dug themselves up from a past life?

Chapter Forty

Did You Ever See A Dream Walking?

Doctor Marchand worked for a prestigious drug company as an inhouse inventor, researcher, and board member. His skills in medicine and science were well matched by his ability to tell jokes and stories. We had the good fortune to meet this gentle and loving man while studying a very subtle form of Buddhism. Every week we would look forward to a relaxed encounter, sit on comfortable thick pillows, and tell the others of our lives and how the principals we were studying helped us fulfill our destinies. Master Sen, the guru, called these meetings "Dharma." Each nuance of the classes was bathed in gentle wisdom. We always began with the sound of an exquisite gong tapped in an ancient rhythm.

Doctor Marchand's turn had come to speak. In his inimitable manner, we awaited what always seemed to become the highlight of each Dharma session. His stories were unabashedly the best. Told with love and humility, our special classmate began a tale that spanned millennia and dimensions.

"I was sound asleep and dreaming. In the dream I saw many alleys and an oriental Casbah bazaar-like environment. There were so many products being sold I was overwhelmed. Even the food had aromas. Everything was so vivid and clear that I decided to touch what the merchants were bartering. In my dream I could feel the leathers and pretty cloths, smell the aromas, taste the foods, hear the music, and see as if I was in the midst of the scenes being presented to me, and was alive. My mouth could speak an ancient tongue to the merchants which was recognizable, but had no name. Although I did not know the country this market place was located in, all seemed to point to somewhere exotically oriental, and fairly wealthy.

The attire worn was that of a warmer or moderate climate. Clothes were loose fitting and extremely colorful. Men wore earrings as did the women. Interestingly, some of them were adorned with as much make-up on their faces as were the females. Not everyone wore make-up though. Those who did, had more jewelry on than the people without face make-up. Their long pampered hair was dark and sometimes braided.

I continued wandering around the maze of alleys and streets until arriving at an open space in the city. Ahead loomed a hill leading into a more mountainous area. Looking up on the hill I saw a beautiful home. With curiosity and a sense of belonging I walked towards the house passing gardens that were abundant with fruits and vegetables. The place was almost royal, very large and well laid out for many to live in, and it had no windows. Instead, the openings in the walls were large enough to climb in and out of almost like a door. Pretty cloth covered these openings. On the floors were ceramic tiles with intricate designs. It felt like home. Many servants scurried around in a great hurry doing their assigned chores. I counted fifteen people before I arrived in an area that contained cooking facilities. This is where I worked. I was a slave.

Deciding to look at myself for the first time in this dream, I found a boy not more than nine or ten. He was a mass of scars, fresh wounds, and hurts. Such a young child to have to be beaten so mercilessly shocked me. At one point I even told myself that this was only a dream. The scenario continued on.

A very tall, fat man walked into the kitchen. He frightened me and I started to shake.

This was the majordomo, butler-in-charge-guy.... who ran the household for our mistress. He sent me to serve her food and drink. Still trembling, I accidentally spilled something on our mistress. In a flash I was back in the kitchen. The fat man began his ritual beating of my head and scarred, slender back. Long ago as a baby, I had learned to mentally leave my body when he did this and faint. This time I did not pass out. I died.

Looking back on this memory, it was a merciful act of kindness to have died. The beatings were actually that of my own ancient father, who obviously was vicious and sadistic. These were inhumane times, and it was a slave society that allowed such behaviors. The woman who had been my mother never survived childbirth. How lucky she was. Her agony ended with my lowly beginnings.

I have experienced this dream ten times. It is always the same. Finally I decided to take trips to search for this mysterious location. There were long and tedious travels to many lands that could possibly have housed that young male slave. One day I hit pay dirt. Walking along an ugly street I found a winding area that resembled my dream. As I meandered in and out of alleys, it dawned on me that this was a very dangerous neighborhood. No matter. The hunt for my ancient roots completely overcame all fears. Certainly, I instinctively had knowledge of these winding streets. After a while an old solid wall all but smashed me in the face, which signalled a complete dead end. This was not the way my dream unfolded at all. What went wrong?

Being an analytical person, I decided to do some intense research. This area could have once been a market place. Obviously, it had long ago deteriorated into a nearly deserted slum. But where did the solid wall come from? Looking through the historical archives was dirty, dusty work for me to do. The museum curator was most generous in allowing my supervised use of their ancient records. This was a very old city with an incredibly well documented written history. After a week of delving, we finally found plans indicating what this place had looked like in the middle ages. It showed the construction of the solid wall. Actually, the wall had really been attached to a huge house. This had long since crumbled, leaving its last remaining thick wall as a reminder of a once proud existence.

But that still did not explain the hill, mountains, and large home where the boy had been a scullery slave. I asked the patient curator how I could bypass the thick wall that was blocking my view in order to continue on with the search. He located a present day street map of the area and it really helped. In order to bypass the wall and move on I had to go many blocks out of the way. Again that deja vu sensation arose in my gut. There was the hill. Not quite as I remembered it, but there just the same and surrounded by those mountains. This is it and now I must find the house where I was murdered. Or, so I thought. Not a trace remained. I walked to where the gardens would have been but it was devoid of anything that could trigger memories. On past the gardens to where the ancient house would have stood. Nothing. Not a shred of evidence was left that could prove my ten identical dreams to have been one of recalling an ancient brief snuffed out life of slavery. I left in frustration thinking I might have made the entire drama up in my own mind.

For some reason I found myself back in the museum emotionally telling all to the curator. He asked me to follow him to a special place where unexplained artifacts were being stored for protection. Rummaging through a box of antiquities, I glimpsed an exquisite ceramic tile. On the artfully executed remnant of an ancient and historically misty time, was the exact design I had seen on the floor tiles in my repeated dream. In a semi-frantic manner I continued going through the box. Then I found proof for my soul of the little boy's existence. The mottled metalic urn I had brought out to serve my mistress with was lying inside this box.

All my life I've had an aversion to serving people. It has been a difficult and personal unhealed phobia of mine. Yet, I'm considered a gourmet cook by all my friends. I'll joyfully conjure up lobster-pot sized meals, but "Serve yourselves" is my motto. This never made any sense to me until learning about the little boy who was beaten to death for spilling food on his mistress."

Chapter Forty One

Irene Was My Mother's Name

In a lifetime of researching and exploring the much disputed phenomena we call "parapsychology" I have not yet met anyone to equal her direct hits. Mom's skill came naturally and was never studied or enhanced by tutors. In fact, she grew up with an extremely superstitious mother. All the gifts and talents she could have further manifested in this arena were disapproved of and thwarted by such an ignorant, fearful environment. Irene's accuracy was impeccable. Details of accidents to come, telepathy, clairvoyance, clair-audience, and minute pieces of information such as foreign addresses of remote places she'd never been to, were everyday fare for her.

She was undoubtedly born in the wrong era for her gift to have been a success. So Irene stayed silently and frustratedly "in the closet" all her life. She would have been burned at the stake during the Inquisition, as well as in Salem. In ancient Greece, Irene might have been a revered oracle and sorceress in a society we still admire in present times. If she had become a medical doctor today, her skill in diagnosing through seeing the aura would have had some spotty recognition, but again might have had to staunchly remain "in the closet" for the majority of her medical peers. There are many societies who used people with these abilities to their great advantage. Healers abound throughout history. You only have to read our bibles to recognize the names.

Yet.... other cultures would simply exterminate them and convince themselves they were doing something rightous.

Can it be that in the vast reaches of our species' mental heritage, we used to communicate through telepathy prior to having language? In still living present day "stone age people" we can find scientifically attested to undeniable use of telepathy in their everyday lives. Why is this aspect of our modern minds still so gravely misunderstood?

Granted, most of the technological societies have submerged our instinctual knowledge in order to worship machines that do our thinking and work. But many have not forgotten what was once the natural heritage of us all. Is telepathy, along with all our additional native Extra Sensory Perceptual abilities to be feared, or a natural aspect of mind that should be re-explored and made to work for the mutual good? Mankind's intuitive selves have been premeditatively subdued and punished nearly out of existence.

You only have to see a flight pattern of birds to know that they are communicating mentally. It's the same with a school of fish. My simple and sincere question is, "Have we evolved or devolved?" If our youngsters were to be sensitivity trained at early ages to listen to their intuition and revere their minds more, could we possibly see increased cures for diseases, as well as more in the way of miraculous inventions? What valuable learnings and accomplishments are we losing because most people no longer respect this aspect of our minds' abilities to hone in on higher information than just logic and technology? We invite your commentaries, and will be sincerely grateful for your input.

FREE DETAILED CATALOGUE

Capall Bann is owned and run by people actively involved in many of the areas in which we publish. A detailed illustrated catalogue is available on request, SAE or International Postal Coupon appreciated. **Titles can be ordered direct from Capall Bann, post free in the UK** (cheque or PO with order) or from good bookshops and specialist outlets.

Do contact us for details on the latest releases at: **Capall Bann Publishing, Auton Farm, Milverton, Somerset, TA4 1NE.** Titles include:

A Breath Behind Time, Terri Hector
Arthur - The Legend Unveiled, C Johnson & E Lung
Astrology The Inner Eye - A Guide in Everyday Language, E Smith
Auguries and Omens - The Magical Lore of Birds, Yvonne Aburrow
Asyniur - Womens Mysteries in the Northern Tradition, S McGrath
Between Earth and Sky, Julia Day
Caer Sidhe - Celtic Astrology and Astronomy, Vol 1, Michael Bayley
Caer Sidhe - Celtic Astrology and Astronomy, Vol 2 M Bayley
Call of the Horned Piper, Nigel Jackson
Cat's Company, Ann Walker
Celtic Faery Shamanism, Catrin James
Celtic Lore & Druidic Ritual, Rhiannon Ryall
Celtic Saints and the Glastonbury Zodiac, Mary Caine
Circle and the Square, Jack Gale
Compleat Vampyre - The Vampyre Shaman, Nigel Jackson
Creating Form From the Mist - The Wisdom of Women in Celtic Myth and
    Culture, Lynne Sinclair-Wood
Crystal Clear - A Guide to Quartz Crystal, Jennifer Dent
Crystal Doorways, Simon & Sue Lilly
Crossing the Borderlines - Guising, Masking & Ritual Animal Disguise in the
    European Tradition, Nigel Pennick
Dragons of the West, Nigel Pennick
Earth Dance - A Year of Pagan Rituals, Jan Brodie
Earth Harmony - Places of Power, Holiness & Healing, Nigel Pennick
Earth Magic, Margaret McArthur
Eildon Tree (The) Romany Language & Lore, Michael Hoadley
Enchanted Forest - The Magical Lore of Trees, Yvonne Aburrow
Eternal Priestess, Sage Weston
Eternally Yours Faithfully, Roy Radford & Evelyn Gregory
Everything You Always Wanted To Know About Your Body, But So Far

Brittany Ferries
FREEPOST (LE6536)
Barwell
LEICESTER
LE9 7BZ

No stamp
required

"Help me find what I'm looking for..."

Choose up to 3 brochures

☐ **French Collection Holidays**
Gîtes • Cottages • Hotels
Holiday Villages • Apartments • Villas
Campsites • River Cruisers

☐ **Spanish Collection Holidays**
Casas • Apartments • Hotels
Paradores • Villas • Campsites
Car Tours • Walks • Portugal

☐ **Ferry Guide France & Spain**
Cruise and high speed services
Price guide • Timetables

☐ **Selected Breaks France & Spain**
Brittany • Normandy • The Loire • Paris
Poitou Charentes • Northern Spain

☐ **Golf Breaks France & Spain**
Brittany • Normandy • Western Loire
Aquitaine • Poitou Charentes
Northern Spain

Which region are you planning to visit?

(tick one only)

☐ Brittany ☐ Normandy ☐ Atlantic Coast
☐ South West ☐ Other ☐ More than one

Title _____ Initials _____

Surname _____

Address _____

_____

Postcode _____

Email Address _____

_____

☐ Please send me regular information by email.

☐ Tick here if you do not want to receive details of
future offers from Brittany Ferries by post.

Just tear off and return this card

Nobody's Been Able To Tell You, Chris Thomas & D Baker
Face of the Deep - Healing Body & Soul, Penny Allen
Fairies in the Irish Tradition, Molly Gowen
Familiars - Animal Powers of Britain, Anna Franklin
Fool's First Steps, (The) Chris Thomas
Forest Paths - Tree Divination, Brian Harrison, Ill. S. Rouse
From Past to Future Life, Dr Roger Webber
Gardening For Wildlife Ron Wilson
God Year, The, Nigel Pennick & Helen Field
Goddesses, Guardians & Groves, Jack Gale
Handbook For Pagan Healers, Liz Joan
Handbook of Fairies, Ronan Coghlan
Healing Book, The, Chris Thomas and Diane Baker
Healing Homes, Jennifer Dent
Healing Journeys, Paul Williamson
Healing Stones, Sue Philips
Herb Craft - Shamanic & Ritual Use of Herbs, Lavender & Franklin
In Search of Herne the Hunter, Eric Fitch
Intuitive Journey, Ann Walker Isis - African Queen, Akkadia Ford
Journey Home, The, Chris Thomas
Kecks, Keddles & Kesh - Celtic Lang & The Cog Almanac, Bayley
Language of the Psycards, Berenice
Legend of Robin Hood, The, Richard Rutherford-Moore
Lid Off the Cauldron, Patricia Crowther
Lore of the Sacred Horse, Marion Davies
Lost Lands & Sunken Cities (2nd ed.), Nigel Pennick
Magic of Herbs - A Complete Home Herbal, Rhiannon Ryall
Magical Guardians - Exploring the Spirit and Nature of Trees, Philip Heselton
Magical History of the Horse, Janet Farrar & Virginia Russell
Magical Lore of Animals, Yvonne Aburrow
Magical Lore of Cats, Marion Davies
Magical Lore of Herbs, Marion Davies
Magick Without Peers, Ariadne Rainbird & David Rankine
Medicine For The Coming Age, Lisa Sand MD
Medium Rare - Reminiscences of a Clairvoyant, Muriel Renard
Mind Massage - 60 Creative Visualisations, Marlene Maundrill
Mirrors of Magic - Evoking the Spirit of the Dewponds, P Heselton
Moon Mysteries, Jan Brodie
Mysteries of the Runes, Michael Howard
Mystic Life of Animals, Ann Walker
Patchwork of Magic - Living in a Pagan World, Julia Day
Pathworking - A Practical Book of Guided Meditations, Pete Jennings
Personal Power, Anna Franklin
Places of Pilgrimage and Healing, Adrian Cooper
Practical Divining, Richard Foord
Practical Meditation, Steve Hounsome

Practical Spirituality, Steve Hounsome
Psychic Self Defence - Real Solutions, Jan Brodie
Real Fairies, David Tame
Reality - How It Works & Why It Mostly Doesn't, Rik Dent
Romany Tapestry, Michael Houghton
Sacred Animals, Gordon MacLellan
Sacred Celtic Animals, Marion Davies, Ill. Simon Rouse
Sacred Dorset - On the Path of the Dragon, Peter Knight
Sacred Grove - The Mysteries of the Forest, Yvonne Aburrow
Sacred Geometry, Nigel Pennick
Sacred Nature, Ancient Wisdom & Modern Meanings, A Cooper
Sacred Ring - Pagan Origins of British Folk Festivals, M. Howard
Secret Places of the Goddess, Philip Heselton
Self Enlightenment, Mayan O'Brien
Spirits of the Earth, Jaq D Hawkins
Stony Gaze, Investigating Celtic Heads John Billingsley
Stumbling Through the Undergrowth , Mark Kirwan-Heyhoe
Subterranean Kingdom, The, revised 2nd ed, Nigel Pennick
Symbols of Ancient Gods, Rhiannon Ryall
Talking to the Earth, Gordon MacLellan
Taming the Wolf - Full Moon Meditations, Steve Hounsome
Teachings of the Wisewomen, Rhiannon Ryall
The Other Kingdoms Speak, Helena Hawley
Tree: Essence of Healing, Simon & Sue Lilly
Tree: Essence, Spirit & Teacher, Simon & Sue Lilly
Through the Veil, Peter Paddon
Vortex - The End of History, Mary Russell
Warp and Weft - In Search of the I-Ching, William de Fancourt
Warriors at the Edge of Time, Jan Fry
Way of the Magus, Michael Howard
Wildwitch - The Craft of the Natural Psychic, Poppy Palin
Wildwood King , Philip Kane
Witches of Oz, Matthew & Julia Philips
Wondrous Land - The Faery Faith of Ireland by Dr Kay Mullin
Working With the Merlin, Geoff Hughes
Your Talking Pet, Ann Walker

FREE detailed catalogue and FREE 'Inspiration' magazine
Contact: Capall Bann Publishing, Auton Farm, Milverton, Somerset, TA4 1NE